Contents

Introduction

Gardening may be as popular as ever, but our towns and cities were not always planned with the needs of gardeners in mind. Few people these days enjoy the luxury of acres of rolling lawns or the gardeners to maintain them – and most of us have to make do with tiny, oddly shaped back gardens, paved patios, balconies, roof terraces, courtyards sandwiched between high buildings or even just a couple of window boxes. At first sight creating a green paradise out of a few square yards of concrete might seem a daunting prospect, but with imagination and know-how even the most unpromising

dark corner can be transformed into a garden of delight, offering a place of repose amid the bustle of daily life.

Making your dream garden in less than ideal surroundings presents its own set of problems, all of

which can be solved with careful planning. First of all, it is a very good idea to decide just what you want out of your garden – whether you want to use it as an extension of the house, for entertaining, as a place for the children to play, as somewhere to

Gardening on a Small Scale

Gardening on a Small Scale

FRASER STEWART

This edition published by
Fraser Stewart Book Wholesale Ltd.
Abbey Chambers
4 Highbridge Street
Waltham Abbey
Essex EN9 1DQ

Produced by Marshall Cavendish Books,
a division of Marshall Cavendish
Partworks Ltd.
119 Wardour Street
London W1V 3TD

© Marshall Cavendish 1993

ISBN 1 85435 5651

Some of this material has previously
appeared in the Marshall Cavendish
Partwork *MY GARDEN*

enjoy snatched moments of solitary tranquillity or as a showcase for your favourite exotic plants. Function will to some extent dictate your priorities, and you will find plenty of ideas for various design approaches in this book to suit any budget.

When space is at a premium, you need to ensure that it is used to the full. Planting will have to be thought out well in advance to ensure that there is something of interest all year round; in a small garden plants really have to prove their worth.

The needs of the plants will also have to be matched with the soil and light conditions. It is also worth considering how much time you have to devote to the garden; if you do not want to spend hours mowing the lawn it might be worth looking at easy maintenance options such as gravel gardens or paving, and plants that require little attention.

Then it is a case of thinking creatively about the available space. If all you have is a balcony or roof terrace, you can still create an entire garden using only container-grown plants in wooden barrels, pots and window boxes. You do not

Introduction *(continued)*

have to restrict yourself to well-tried annuals; many vegetables and herbs do well in containers. Similarly, a garden that gets very little sun is no cause for despair; many plants positively flourish in these conditions and you can make a green retreat using shade-lovers like ferns, or brighten up dark corners with woodland flowers such as primroses or Solomon's seal. If you nurture a secret ambition to design picturesque vistas but only have a back yard surrounded by high walls, you can still create an entire landscape in miniature using small plants in an old sink or a scree bed or rockery. If you hanker after the sound of running water but a full-size pond or stream is out of the question, you can create a delightful water garden in a tub complete with a small fountain. And if you do not have the space for a full-size orchard, this book will tell you how to get the best out of espaliered or cordoned-trained fruit trees.

However imaginative you are you still need practical know-how to turn your dream into reality. This book will give you invaluable hints on how to grow successfully in limited space; how to plant up your containers and hanging baskets; how to make raised beds; how to train your climbing plants up wigwams or trellises and the right compost to choose and when to feed and water. You will also find helpful suggestions about which plants are right for which conditions, and how to combine them for the best results. Then all you will have to do is relax and enjoy the fruit of your labours!

Front Door Containers

Your doorway is the 'face' that your household presents to the world. You can make it welcoming and beautiful all year round by using containers.

The entrance to your house can be welcoming, forbidding or just plain dull, depending on what you do with it.

Every year, in spring and early summer, doorways are enlivened by the sudden appearance of hanging baskets, tubs and pots, filled to bursting with vibrant colour. Even some of the most reluctant gardeners respond to this annual call for colour.

This stunning display does not have to be just an annual event; there is not need to consign your tubs and pots to the shed at the end of the summer. With a little planning, your front door containers can earn their keep all year round.

Choosing what to put in your containers in spring and summer is not difficult; there is such a wealth of possibilities. Autumn and winter, however, can be a problem for the inexperienced gardener.

New life

Late winter is a dreary time. Gardens tend to be bare and we long for the first signs of new life to appear. One of the joys of containers at your door is that you can watch for these signs of life in comfort.

One of the best ways to provide permanence at your door is to plant a tree in a tub.

This doorway, festooned above and below with summer colour from tubs, hanging baskets and pots, makes a stunning display.

9

MAKING A MARK

It can be very annoying when you are planting bedding plants to disturb bulbs that are already there.

When you are planting your bulbs, put a little sand on top of them before filling in with soil or compost. Then, when you are planting other things, the sight of sand will warn you to dig carefully because there are bulbs around.

However, a small tree has really got to earn its keep if it is to be given tub-room. It really must be able to provide you with more than one area or season of interest.

Choosing a tree

The sweet bay (*Laurus nobilis*) provides dark, glossy evergreen leaves, a pleasing shape when clipped and aromatic leaves for use in the kitchen.

A small Japanese maple will have a good shape, interesting summer foliage and glorious

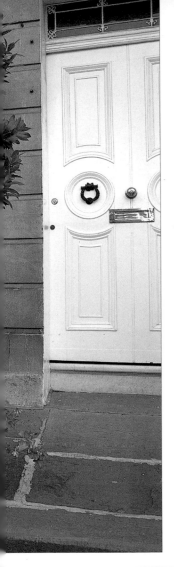

Acer palmatum 'Dissectum Atropurpureum' (far left) provides glorious autumn foliage.

A classic bay tree (above left), is given added interest with colourful underplanting.

Welcoming petunias and lobelia (left) in a front door tub.

A container garden (above) enlivens an otherwise dull door.

autumn colour. *Acer palmatum* 'Dissectum Atropurpureum' is a good choice, but it must have a sheltered position and protection from late frosts.

Ballerina apple trees are useful in an all-year-round tub. True, their columnar shape is unexciting, but they have buds in early spring, blossom a little later and apples in the autumn. Their shape does have its advan-

POTS FOR ALL SEASONS

To save yourself the trouble of constantly uprooting and replanting at the end of each season, simply have a selection of containers planted for a succession of interest. Swap the containers when necessary and store the out-of-season ones in the garden or in a shed for next year.

You could have a display of winter heathers and dwarf conifers for the depths of winter. In the spring you could replace it with pots of bulbs. Summer bedding must be done annually but autumn bulbs can just be brought out when needed.

In this way your front door need never be without a container brimming with life and colour to welcome visitors.

BRIGHT IDEAS

11

PLANTS FOR AUTUMN

There are a few plants that are at their best in late summer and autumn. *Coleus* varieties have lovely foliage and will last in your tub until the first frosts. Discard them then or lift them earlier and store them overwinter as houseplants. Choose 'Brightness' for rust-coloured leaves with a glorious light green edging. 'Fashion Parade' has multi-coloured leaves of various shapes. For a very wide selection of leaf colours, choose the Wizard Series.

Fatsia japonica has handsome evergreen leaves and white flowers in autumn.

Autumn bulbs will provide flowers. *Nerine bowdenii* is suitable for mild areas (it needs a sheltered position) and provides wonderfully delicate pink blooms. The *alba* form has white flowers with a subtle pink flush.

Various *Cyclamen* will flower in autumn. Choose *C. hederifolium* for pink flowers and the *album* variety for pure white. *C. mirabile* is pink with a purple stain at the mouth.

Colchicum 'Waterlily' is a lovely autumn flower in a stunning pink; for white choose *C. speciosum* 'Album'. *C. autumnale* comes in pink, white or purple. *C. byzantinum* has open, pale purplish-pink flowers.

Mauves and purples can be provided by some of the crocus family. *Crocus nudiflorus* is a rich purple. *C. banaticus* is a pale violet and has an unusual shape for a crocus. *C. speciosus* 'Oxonian' is a deep blue-purple with a gorgeous orange stigma.

Sternbergia lutea looks like a crocus and is a bright yellow, a welcome change from pink, white and purple.

Check your garden centre for pansies that flower in autumn; there are now varieties for every season.

tages; the lack of spreading branches allows you to under-plant them with bulbs and bedding plants.

Ballerina trees tend to be a little dull in summer because their leaves are not dramatic, but you could grow an annual climber up them to provide temporary interest. Climbing nasturtiums, sweet peas or morning glory are all useful for this purpose.

Plants for winter

Unfortunately, there is no really suitable climber to give interest in the depths of winter after deciduous trees have lost their leaves. Ivy is a possibility, but it is likely to take over very quickly and smother your trees in time. It is better to provide winter interest by clever under-planting.

The development of Uni-

versal pansies, which flower in winter, is a real boon for winter hanging baskets, tubs and pots. You can plant them under a tub-grown tree or you can devote whole pots and baskets to them. Pansies look best when planted in bold groups.

Add some trailing ivy or *Glechoma hederacea* 'Variegata' to soften the edges and provide an interesting, leafy contrast.

Polyanthus are perennials, often treated as biennials, and the variety 'Crescendo' will flower in winter. You can use these charming plants to underplant your tree; add some attactive trailers to complete the picture.

Another way to create a stunning winter container is to adopt the Victorians' method of winter bedding. They plunged pots of small evergreen shrubs in beds and borders to provide winter interest. The pots were lifted each year and stored in an out-of-the-way spot to make room for spring and summer bedding.

You can do the same but on a much smaller scale. A pot containing a small conifer or any one of a number of suitable evergreens can be plunged into your tub as a centrepiece, surrounded by winter flowers and trailers. If you need the planting space in spring, simply lift the pot and store it ready for re-planting in the autumn months.

Beautiful bulbs

There are bulbs for all seasons and many of them are happy to live in containers. The winter aconite (*Eranthis hyemalis*) will produce buttercup yellow flowers from late winter to early spring.

Outdoor cyclamens will all tolerate frost and will flower in winter. Choose *C. coum* 'Album', which has white flowers with a fetching maroon mark at the mouth. Or try *C. coum coum*; its deep carmine flowers have dark stains at the mouth. Sometimes the leaves of both types have silver markings for added winter interest.

Fancy-leaved and ivy-leaved pelargoniums cascade from a pedestal container (above left), making an appropriately romantic entrance to an old house with flagstone paving and heavy wooden door.

For a truly grand and unusual door display, ivy can be potted in an elegant container and trained into a conifer shape (far left).

This front-door porch (above) features potted lilies, fatsia and ivies held together with gnarled wood.

When their summer flowering is over, brightly-coloured baskets (left) can be planted with equally cheerful winter-flowering pansies.

Shrubs in Tubs

If it's a formal look you're after, clipped bay trees by the front door, shaped yew on the patio, and upright conifers on the balcony will add a touch of class to even the smallest garden.

Formal shrubs in tubs do not belong only in grand gardens. They are often at their most effective in relatively modest spaces where they have lots of impact. In a very small town garden, a patio, balcony or roof garden, a few formal container shrubs will add welcome greenery and real character.

Many informal shrubs – those with a loose outline or spreading profile, such as Japanese mapes and the false castor oil plant – make excellent container shrubs. It is the crisp, geometric outline of formal shrubs, however, that makes them especially useful as focal-point plants or for creating a sense of design and structure in a garden.

Bold statements
You can, of course, grow formal shrubs in the ground, but planted among other shrubs they often lose some of their impact, and you cannot move them around at will, as you can when they are in containers.

You can place these potted shrubs where their very unexpectedness is an attraction – by the front porch, or on a balcony for instance.

Pot panache
The containers, too, make a vital contribution. By raising a shrub off the ground and presenting it in splendid isolation, they actually enhance the plant. As formal shrubs are usually evergreen, and most will be grown for foliage effect, a container that has a bold or intricate design will add another element of interest.

Hanging Baskets

Create a lovely visual effect with a beautiful basket that can be hung wherever you need a splash of summer colour. You can buy ready-planted baskets from a garden centre, but it is much more fun to plant your own.

Hanging baskets can be used to brighten up a bare wall, giving a view of flowers and foliage from windows that would otherwise face only bricks. They can make a 'garden' on the side of a house or dreary back yard where there is no room to grow any plants at ground level.

Hanging baskets can be suspended from a pergola to give a floral walkway down a garden path or across a patio. They are especially good in this instance, to add summer colour when the climbers grown on the pergola flower early or late in the season and have little to offer except foliage in high summer.

What sort of basket?

Traditionally, hanging baskets were made from galvanized wire and would be lined with sphagnum moss. Nowadays black polythene is often used instead of, or together with, the moss. The major advantage in using moss is that it is more attractive than black plastic.

A third alternative is to buy ready-made moulded liners of compressed peat and fibre which can be placed straight into your basket.

The basket itself is usually made from plastic or wire and can either be meshed or solid. The main advantage of mesh baskets, is, of course, that plants can be inserted through the gaps, making a spectacular display. Solid baskets,

Basketworks: enliven a wall clad with green leafy climbers (above) by adding a softly coloured basket arrangement; use a riot of red against pale brickwork (above left); a porch is the perfect place to hang a showpiece basket (left).

Clay pots (far left), painted to match the front door, make ideal containers for the variegated Aucuba japonica 'Maculata'. The effect is stylish yet unimposing and provides the finishing touch to an enclosed porch.

These bay trees (right) have been trained into tall columns and are being used to frame an unusual arched window. The stylish elegance is reflected in the smart white painted wooden 'Versailles' tubs.

For a less constrained, yet still formal approach, this bay tree has been left to grow naturally. The softer outline compliments the country charm of the cottage.

For quick and dependable results, keep to widely available, reliable plants to achieve the desired effect.

What to grow

Bay (*Laurus nobilis*) responds well to formal clipping, and is ideal to use in pairs by the front or back door. There is also the bonus of bay leaves for the kitchen – but do not raid the plant too often or you will spoil its shape.

There is just one major drawback with bay; it is not reliably hardy. In mild areas, it will survive most winters unharmed, but it is not a good choice in cold districts, especially as container plants are more vulnerable to frosts.

Box (*Buxus sempervirens*) thrives on formal clipping, and is really tough. You can buy ready-clipped pyramids from good nurseries and garden centres, though you will still have to keep it trimmed.

If you want to train your

own (which is much cheaper), buy a tall-growing variety. 'Handsworthensis' is a good one, or choose the variegated 'Aureovariegata' for a lighter, more colourful look.

Privet is cheap, tough, and quick-growing – all of which makes it a good one to try if you want to start training your own plants. You will need to clip it frequently as it can become unruly, and it lacks the elegance that some of the more 'classic' plants possess, but a golden privet will bring colour to a dull corner in a way that other traditional green formal shrubs cannot.

Shrubby honeysuckle (*Lonicera nitida*), not to be confused with the climbing group of honeysuckles, is another inexpensive plant that clips well to a formal shape. It is unlikely that these will be available as ready-trained specimens, but they are widely sold as hedging plants, and it is easy to clip them to almost any shape. There is a golden form that is particularly attractive, 'Baggesen's Gold'.

Cutting style

Yew is a favourite topiary plant, but it does not generally do so well as a container plant. You can, however, sometimes buy ready trained container-

It is worth standing a particularly fine specimen of a tender shrub such as this Heptapleureum arboricola 'Variegata' (above) on the patio for the summer. Keep such plants indoors during the winter months or they will be killed by frosts.
A sleek conifer (right) with its tall, narrow shape creates a distinctive focal point near a window or doorway. This easy-to-care-for shrub makes it a practical choice.

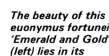

The beauty of this euonymus fortunei 'Emerald and Gold' (left) lies in its delicately patterned foliage. Colourful all year round, it is the perfect addition to a patio, path, balcony or any area that needs brightening up. It can be trimmed into shape using shears if a more formal look is desired.

grown topiary specimens.

If you want to experiment, and save money at the same time, start with something easy to train like a holly or the winter-flowering bushy evergreen *Viburnum tinus*.

You are unlikely to buy these ready-trained, but if you do not mind waiting a few years, the results will be impressive (hollies in particular can be very slow growing). Both of these plants are widely available in garden centres.

To keep faster growing formal shrubs in shape, clip them with shears as frequently as necessary – this may be as much as several times in one growing season.

Plants with larger leaves

Box (left) is the ideal shrub for clipping and this one has been trimmed into a lovely ball shape. The simplicity of the pot complements the rounded outlines. Similarly, this beautiful bay (right) has been trained into an ellipse and its formal oval outline contrasts well with the easy country charm of a wooden barrel.

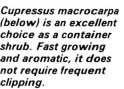

Cupressus macrocarpa (below) is an excellent choice as a container shrub. Fast growing and aromatic, it does not require frequent clipping.

FIVE FAVOURITES

● Box (*Buxus sempervirens*). Small, leathery, dark green leaves. Variegated varieties available. Easily clipped.

● Bay (*Laurus nobilis*). Large, leathery green leaves. The beauty lies in the formal shaping. Trained specimens are widely available.

● Privet (*ligustrum*). Try a golden variety for a brighter look. Easily clipped to shape.

● Shrubby honeysuckle (*Lonicera nitida*). Small green leaves, and quick growth. Easy to train; but requires frequent clipping.

● Yew (*taxus baccata*). Tolerates close clipping.

GARDEN NOTES

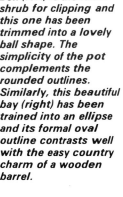

should not be clipped with shears, however.

The least expensive choice for a grow-your-own formal container plant is a conifer. Many grow naturally into an attractive oval or cone, without any trimming. Because many are relatively quick-growing, they are also usually inexpensive. You can buy fairly large container-grown specimens for much less than you would pay for other trained evergreens of similar size. They need not be boring either: try golden forms, or those with unusual blue-grey foliage.

Not all conifers do well in containers, however. Some cannot tolerate dry roots, which is a hazard for container plants if you forget to water regularly in dry spells.

Choosing containers

A generous amount of good compost is essential if your shrub is to thrive in a container. Similarly good drainage is a must. Some plastic shrub tubs come with areas of

SHAPING UP

Pencil column

Pyramid shape

'Lollipop'

Oval outline

Buy plants ready-trained for stunning effects. Use shears for small leaved plants and secateurs for larger leaves.

thin plastic that have to be punched out to create drainage holes. Any container which is less than 30cm/12in in diameter is unlikely to be suitable for a tree or shrub; ideally 45cm/18in is the minimum size unless the plant is still very small.

Plastic tubs are practical and inexpensive but generally do not look very imposing.

Imitation stone (sometimes known as reconstituted stone) is very impressive and an ornamental pot or urn, perhaps with some ornate decoration, or standing on a plinth, is just right for a plant such as a formal clipped bay or a neat specimen conifer.

Frost-proof clay or terracotta pots come in wide variety of shapes and sizes and are ideal for shrubs cut into 'lollipops' or similar shapes as their simplicity will enhance rather than detract from the overall effect.

Wooden 'Versailles' tubs, square in shape, are elegant and look especially good containing bay pyramids. Some plastic versions can look very convincing.

Half barrels make ideal shrub tubs. Before you plant anything in them ensure that they have suitable drainage by

Q I have had ... clipped bay ... several years bu... of the leaves loo... brown at the edg...

A The brown... are probab... result of winter... wind burn if it s... a windy or exp... position. Move... sheltered spot... especially in w...

Q I have a ... a pot an... like to add s... seasonal col... plant somethi... the container...

A Try a ... spring... bulbs such... or grape h... a small tra... variegated... the pot is... however,... bedding... deprived... water da... flowers... summer...

WHAT WENT WRONG?

drilling a fe... bottom. You... them white... hoops. The... containers... shrubs.

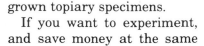 **PLANTING A S...**

1. Place a thick layer of crocks or large gravel in the bottom of the container to improve drainage, remembering that it must also have drainage holes.
2. Add a good loam-based compost to a depth that will bring the root-ball to within about 5cm/2in of the rim of the container. Don't depend on the garden soil. Container plants use a lot of nutrients and the soil probably won't have enough to feed the plant.
3. Remove the shrub from its container, tease out a few large roots, and trickle compost around until it is level with the top of the root-ball. Water well.

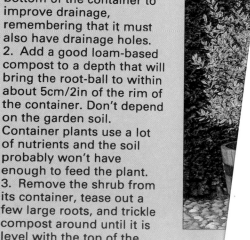

To prev... gravel a...

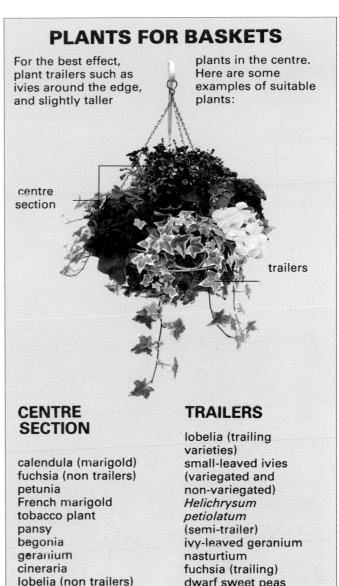
though slightly easier to plant, are often not quite so effective. The solid plastic versions are like large flower pots and usually have rigid plastic wires and a drip saucer attached to the bottom. Others are made from fibre and resemble heavy-duty versions of the peat and fibre liners. These will only last for a couple of seasons, but are inexpensive, look natural and are extremely easy to use.

Making an impact

A wide selection of both flowering and foliage plants makes much more of an impact than just two or three plants of different varieties.

Conversely, try just one kind of plant in a single colour for a really striking effect. Some of the best plants for this are petunias or fibrous-rooted begonias for a sunny position and busy Lizzies or fuchsias for a shady site.

Plan your baskets with your window boxes or other containers in mind; either match them in colour and texture for a harmonious effect or contrast them completely for an equally attractive and very arresting design. Try matching your baskets to complement their surroundings, picking up

LONG-LASTING

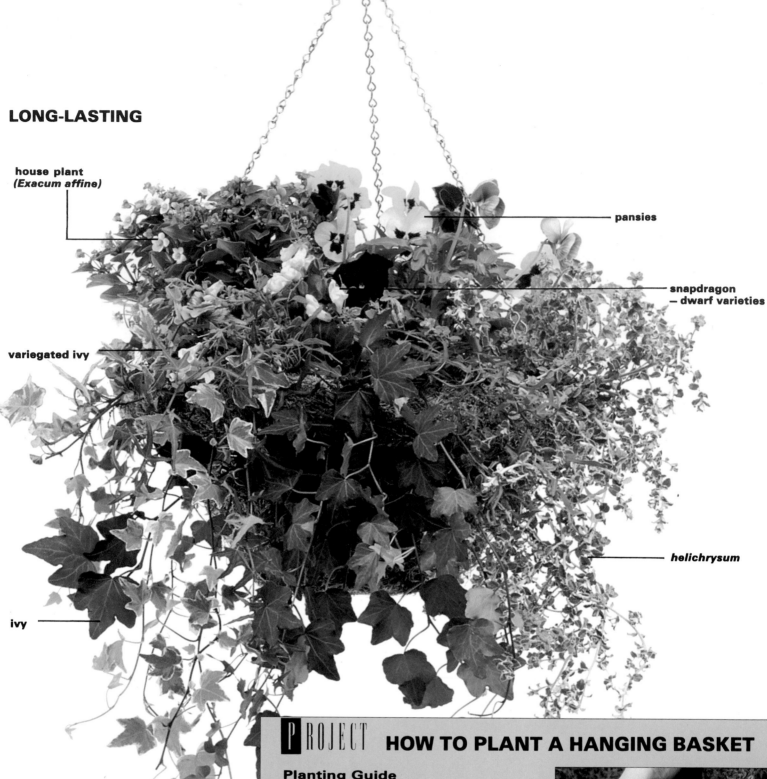

house plant
(*Exacum affine*)

pansies

snapdragon
– dwarf varieties

variegated ivy

helichrysum

ivy

Long-lasting Basket

To fill a basket 25-30cm/10-12in in diameter, you will need approximately four pansies, six ivies (some plain, some variegated), one or two dwarf antirrhinums and three helichrysums.

Choose reasonably mature plants so that you will not have to wait too long for the basket to 'bush out'.

While you are waiting for plants to spread, fill any gaps with small, potted plants that can easily be removed. The *Exacum affine* is really pretty, but tender, so place in an outdoor arrangement only in very mild or sheltered conditions.

This basket will look good all summer long and last well into autumn, until the first frosts.

ℙ ROJECT   HOW TO PLANT A HANGING BASKET

Planting Guide

Stand the basket on an upturned pot to help steady it as you work.

The sphagnum moss should be damp; position it with the greenest parts facing outwards.

Before adding special potting compost, you may like to place an old saucer or a circle cut from a plastic bag in the base of the basket as a further aid to moisture retention and a few lumps of charcoal, which helps to prevent water becoming stagnant.

Firm the roots of plants into the compost as you work. When you have finished planting, stand the basket in a large bowl or container of water until it is thoroughly soaked. Soak once a week thereafter, and water daily using a can with a fine rose.

1 *Place basket on a plant pot and line with damp sphagnum moss. Push trailers through sides.*

BOLD AND BRIGHT

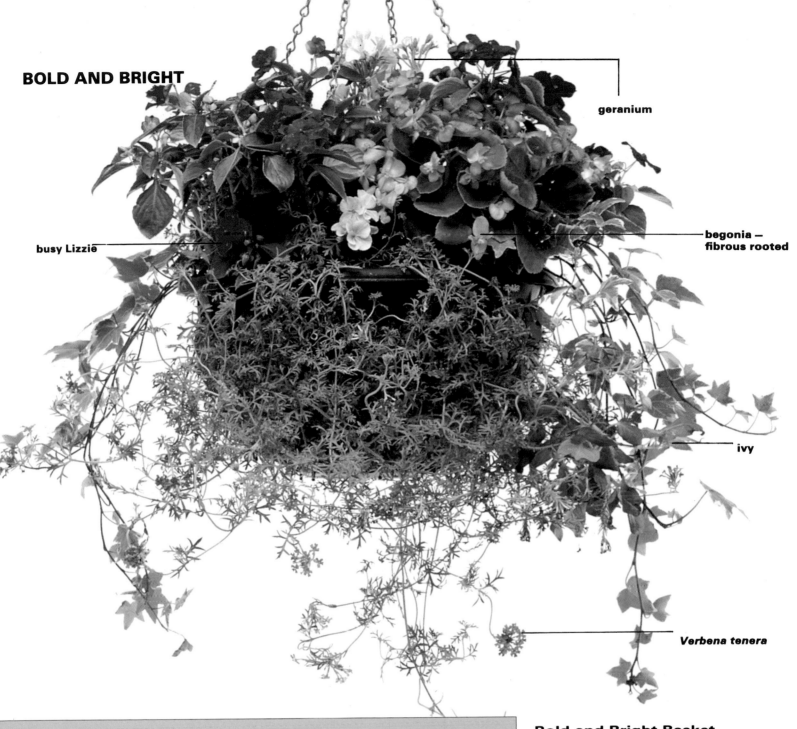

geranium

begonia — fibrous rooted

busy Lizzie

ivy

Verbena tenera

2 Cut a circle of plastic for the base of the basket to aid moisture retention. Arrange the outer rim plants and firm in.

3 Position the central plant, which should stand taller than those surrounding it. Firm in, water the basket and allow to settle and drain before hanging in your chosen location.

Bold and Bright Basket

This basket displays bold and pastel coloured plants in greens and pinks. The two-colour theme makes just as great an impact as baskets with a mass of colours. This selection of plants fills a 25cm/10in basket with a beautiful array of foliage and leaves.

You will need three or four busy Lizzies and the same number of begonias, two small geraniums, about six verbenas and three or four ivies.

Arrange the plants on the surface of this basket before putting in their final positions to show off a balanced display.

Plant the verbenas first, ensuring that they are evenly spaced around the basket, their trailing stems poking through the sides. Follow these with the different ivies.

Finish your basket by planting the busy Lizzies, begonias and geraniums which will form a bushy mass of flowers and foliage on top.

on the colour of your garden pots for example.

A basket filled with moist compost and well-developed plants weighs a considerable amount. It must be hung from a very strong support, on chains, from a bracket screwed either to a wall or to the sides of a doorway, or hung from the underside of a porch, balcony, arch or pergola. You will need to use a drill with a masonry bit to plug the wall before screwing anything to it.

Watering ways

Compost in hanging baskets dries out rapidly in hot weather and needs watering once or even twice a day. An effective way of doing this is to take down the basket and stand it in a bowl of water for 15 minutes or so until the compost is thoroughly damp. This will quickly revive a flagging display. You should not do this, however, if the basket is too heavy or it contains trailing plants which could easily be crushed in the process.

There are special devices available which allow baskets to be lowered on a pulley for easy access. Alternatively, a pump can with a two litre bottle and long tube makes watering easy without lowering, and so does a watering lance fitted on to the end of a garden hose – or try an old washing-up liquid bottle as a cheap option.

Even after heavy bursts of rain baskets may need watering as plant growth may have prevented rain reaching the roots, or house eaves may have kept the rain off all together.

Keep them sweet

When you water your basket, take the opportunity to cut off

A basket (right) full of lobelia and busy Lizzie in brilliant shades of pink with just a few touches of white makes a most attractive, colour-coordinated display.

Make the most of the smallest of garden spaces with lots of flowering baskets. Creating a theme makes a bold statement, such as here, where trailing basket geraniums (below) link prettily with the tub geraniums beneath.

This simple but effective planting scheme (left) uses foliage as much as flowers for its impact. Soft pink trailing geraniums and silvery helichrysums show up particularly well against a dark brick wall.

A newly erected fence can look a bit stark while you're waiting for plants to grow up against it. Just the place to have a hanging basket (left), or even two or three.

the dead heads from flowering plants and, as the season progresses, pinch back any very vigorous plants, such as *Helichrysum petiolatum* or nasturtiums, as they can smother their neighbours if left to grow unchecked.

You may need to remove plants that have died or finished flowering. Rather than leave gaps in the basket, ease some small plants such as fibrous-rooted begonias or violas into the spaces left behind.

Little pests!

Keep a watch out for weeds and remove them at once. You can deter birds from pulling out young plants by pushing a number of short twigs into the compost, then winding black thread, lattice-fashion, around them to create 'netting'.

Aphids (green or black fly) are the most common pests you are likely to encounter. They must be dealt with quickly otherwise they will soon multiply. To avoid using insecticide, spray the aphids forcefully with soapy water and repeat the treatment as necessary.

Bloomin' beautiful

Colour scheming does not have to be confined to the house. Just as you match the colours of carpets, curtains and cushions, let your imagination flow and indulge your creativity by planting baskets which reflect the colours of your garden. Most small plants which will flourish in a container will grow happily in a hanging basket – so use them to the full.

For something really different try growing fruit or vegetables in a basket. Use dwarf or mini tomatoes, or Sweetheart strawberries to make a vibrant display of red and green. Make a herb basket and hang it by the kitchen door so that your fresh supply is near at hand. Fill it with parsley, a mix of silver, gold and green thymes, purple and gold sages and other colourful herbs. Add bright nasturtiums and remember the leaves, flowers and seeds are edible.

Hanging baskets need not be banished in autumn and winter. If kept in a sheltered spot, replace summer displays with small leaved variegated ivies or euonymus. Plant early bulbs like crocuses and snowdrops to welcome the spring and replace these later with coloured primroses, pansies, pot-grown hyacinths or dwarf daffodils – to take you into summer.

Making an Entrance

Create a wonderful first impression by dressing up your doorway with colourful, fragrant and easy-to-grow flowering climbers.

Roses add a touch of romance to country houses. This mature climbing rose has aged with the house, draping the porch in a profusion of blossom and rich, dark foliage.

The extravagant effect created by flowering climbers is so easy to achieve and can transform the whole look of your home. You require only the smallest of spaces – and even if the area surrounding your door is concrete you can still enjoy the beauty of a climber as many will grow perfectly well in pots.

Romance in bloom

Whether you choose roses for their old-fashioned, romantic appeal or clematis for a touch of vibrant colour you may be sure of the maximum effect for the minimum effort and outlay. Roses and clematis are among the most popular climbers because they provide both beautiful and trouble-free blooms year after year.

At garden centres, climbing plants are usually grouped together. Each has its own individual label giving the name, cultivation instructions and eventual height.

Splash out on colour

Clematis is a universal favourite and there is an enormous range of colours to choose from – white, pink, red, blue and lavender, vibrant purple or showy yellow blooms. There are hundreds of varieties available and each garden centre has its own selection.

Most popular are the large-flowered hybrids which are a cross between two varieties. They have round, flat, spectacular blooms, which can be up to 25cm/10in across. Generally they have a single layer of petals, but some are semi-double or even double, like a powder puff or a ballerina's skirt.

Hybrids flower from late spring to autumn, according to variety. Some early types have a second, smaller flush of flowers in summer or autumn; while others can keep flowering for months on end.

'Species' clematis are pure bred and less showy, but easier to grow. Their charming flowers are smaller than hybrids, and can be flat or shaped like cups or bells. They are ideal for creating a cottage-garden effect.

A warm welcome

Climbing roses can put on the most stunning displays of all. The single, semi-double or double flowers come in white and every shade of cream, yellow, orange, pink and red.

Some have petals with contrasting edges or undersides, while others change colour as they develop from tight buds to fully open flowers. Many are deliciously fragrant – even more reason to grow them round a front door.

In garden centres, true

Climbing roses can look equally stunning when grown around the front doors of modern houses. This variety (right) – 'Etoile de Hollande' has a profusion of opulent velvety-red blossoms which contrast with the white paintwork to stunning effect. A particularly fragrant rose, it makes an excellent choice to grace a doorway.

This simple porch (below) has been transformed by a mass of large, open-cupped flowers from the wonderful clematis variety 'Nelly Moser'. The fragile, almost translucent, mauve-pink petals are enhanced by a cheeky pink stripe. The long flowering season of this variety ensures any visitors the brightest of welcomes in late spring and early summer.

climbing roses, which have a permanent woody framework, are often mixed in with rambling roses, whose thin, pliable stems are cut to the ground after flowering each year. If you are unsure whether a rose is a climber or rambler be sure to ask an assistant, so you can receive advice on how to prune it correctly.

No two garden centres will have the same choice of climbing roses, but refer to the list on page 94 for climbing roses most likely to be featured. All those listed are 'repeat flowering', which means they bloom over several months, as opposed to 'non-recurrent' types, which flower magnificently but only for a week or two each year.

Buying climbers

For the widest choice, buy in autumn or early spring, when garden centres receive their new stock. Many reputable garden centres will replace plants which do not 'take' so keep the label, just in case! Always examine plants very carefully. Steer clear of old plants that have outgrown their containers. Such specimens may have difficulty settling in.

Choose plants with two or more strong, sturdy stems, at least 60cm/2ft long. Climbing roses should have dormant buds. Roses are sometimes sold bare-rooted, or pre-packaged, but these can be tricky and are best avoided if

SOLUTIONS FOR SHADY WALLS

If your front door gets little or no direct sunlight, do not despair! You can still grow some climbing roses, including 'Danse du Feu', 'Mme Alfred Carrière' and 'Golden Showers'.

The extremely vigorous Clematis montana can grow up to 12.5m/40ft tall and has a spread of up to 6m/20ft. It is perfectly possible to use a climber as vigorous as this to frame a front door, but it must be kept in check or it may soon outgrow the whole house. Prudent pruning is therefore essential, to produce an attractive framework. It can be trained to form an elegant arch around the door of a town house (left), where pink-tinged flowers have been chosen to set off the bright red paintwork. The perfection of a pure white clematis (below), grown to form a canopy, adds charm to a suburban house and helps to hide an unsightly drainpipe.

THE BEST CLIMBING ROSES

Roses	Height	Features
R. 'Aloha'	2.4m/8ft	Double, rose-pink, hybrid tea-like fragrant flowers
R. 'Etoile de Hollande'	3.5m/12ft	Double, deep-red hybrid tea-like very fragrant flowers
R. 'Danse du Feu'	3m/10ft	Double, orange-scarlet, large flowers; no scent
R. 'Golden Showers'	2.1m/7ft	Large, double, golden-yellow, fragrant flowers
R. 'Handel'	3m/10ft	Large, double, cream flowers, edged deep pink, slightly fragrant
R. 'Mermaid'	8m/25ft	Single, primrose-yellow, fragrant, large flowers
R. 'Mme Alfred Carrière'	6m/20ft	Large, double, fragrant, apricot-orange flowers
R. 'Schoolgirl'	3m/10ft	Large, double, fragrant, creamy-white flowers
R. 'Swan Lake'	2.4m/8ft	Double, white, pink-tinged, slightly fragrant flowers
R. 'Zéphirine Drouhin'	3m/10ft	Deep-pink, semi-double, very fragrant flowers

THE BEST CLEMATIS

Clematis	Height	Features
Clematis alpina	2.4m/8ft	Violet-blue, bell-like spring flowers, silky seed heads
Clematis 'Beauty of Worcester'	2.5m/8ft	Deep violet, double flowers in early summer
Clematis 'Ernest Markham'	3m/10ft	Large petunia-red, flowers, in late summer, autumn
Clematis 'Jackmanii Superba'	3m/10ft	Dark violet-purple, large flowers in summer, autumn
Clematis 'Lasurstern'	3m/10ft	Deep purple-blue flowers from summer to autumn
Clematis montana	12m/40ft	Bears masses of single, white flowers in spring
Clematis 'Nelly Moser'	3m/10ft	Spring-flowering pale pink petals with carmine stripes
Clematis tangutica	3m/10ft	Yellow, lantern-shaped, blooms in late summer
Clematis 'Ville de Lyon'	3m/10ft	Large flowers, edged with crimson in late summer
Clematis 'Vyvyan Pennell'	3m/10ft	Violet-blue, double flowers, from late spring to autumn

R. 'Handel' is a perpetually flowering variety.

R. 'Golden Showers' does not need a sunny aspect.

C. 'Nelly Moser' with its stunning stripes.

C. 'Jackmanii Superba' has velvet-purple flowers.

Plant clematis in complementary colours. The choice above is the unusual moody blue 'Perle d'Azur' and carmine-red flowered 'Ville de Lyon'. Both flower in mid to later summer.

NO PROBLEM!

Q Why did my neighbour lay paving slabs around the base of his clematis when he planted it?

A Although clematis flower best in sun, their roots prefer cool, damp soil. Placing a concrete slab or large stone over the roots does the trick, and also keeps weeds down.

Q My climbing rose now has two types of shoots, the original, plus new ones with smaller leaves, coming from the base. Should I cut them out or leave them?

A The new shoots are suckers, growing from the rootstock of the variety onto which it was originally grafted. If left to grow, they can overtake the named variety, leaving you with inferior flowers. Dig out the soil around the sucker, tracing it back to where it joins the roots. Pull it off, replace the soil and firm in.

you are not an 'expert'.

Plant as soon after buying as you can, as long as the soil is not frozen or waterlogged. Allow at least 37cm/15in space away from the wall, since soil near a wall is unlikely to get much rain.

Make the hole twice as wide and deep as the pot, and fork over the bottom. Place a thick layer of organic compost in the bottom. Water the plant while still in its pot, then carefully remove it and place the root-ball in the centre of the hole, angling canes towards the wall. The top of the root ball should be level with the surrounding soil.

Return the dug-out soil, mixed with a handful of bone meal, to the hole. If your soil is poor, use rich, loam-based potting compost, such as John Innes No 3, instead. Firm in as you then water.

Giving support

Try to fix the climber to the support before planting, so you don't accidentally damage the plant. You can use flexible, mesh netting for small clematis; stronger, rigid, plastic-coated mesh panels; or, prettiest of all, trellis. These come in collapsible or rigid panels, painted wood or plastic. Battens are thin planks which are attached to the wall first.

This rose (above) has been trained to produce a flowering canopy. The delicate peach-coloured flowers pick out the tones of the brickwork.

BE CREATIVE!

● If you grow climbers in a tub, plant spring bulbs and colourful annuals round the main stems, with ivies round the edge for year-round interest.
● For a balanced effect, plant identical climbers either side of the front door.
● Select two different climbers to live together: climbing pink rose and blue or purple clematis, for example, tone beautifully.
● Buy a ready-made ornamental metal or rustic wooden arch, and fix it in front of your door, for instant and attractive support for climbers.

GARDEN NOTES

Fix the supports to these and there will be room for the climbers to weave in and out and for the air to move freely.

Toughened metal vine eyes can be hammered into brick mortar, and galvanized wires stretched horizontally bet-ween them to provide a cheap and unobtrusive support. Place the first wire 90cm/3ft above the ground and then at 23-30cm/9-12in intervals.

Use soft green twine, raffia or plastic-coated wire ties to tie in newly planted climbers; established climbing roses may need stronger, plastic tree ties. Established clematis cling with their leaf tendrils so they need no help.

Prettily contained

Even if your front door is sur-rounded by concrete you can still create a lush effect by growing climbers in large flower pots or tubs. Buy clay pots in plain or ornate styles, or for a cool, formal look, use wooden-style Versailles tubs: some come with tall, pyramid-shaped white trellis attached, for instant, free-standing sup-port. To create a cottage gar-den effect, use old-fashioned beer barrel halves. A large trough can be planted with more than one climber.

The container should be at least 35cm/14in across, so the roots will not dry out in sum-mer or freeze in winter. Put in crocks and fill with a layer of loam-based potting compost.

The wars of the roses may have been fiercely fought in days gone by but here (above) the red rose of Lancaster and the white rose of York are joined in glorious harmony. Make sure you choose roses which flower at the same time of year for a two-colour contrast. The white rose 'Mme Alfred Carrière' and the scarlet

'Danse du Feu' both flower from summer to autumn. For another stunning combination try growing a rose and a clematis together (below). Here, C. 'Hagley Hybrid' with its pretty lilac-pink, large, flat blooms has been grown with an American pillar rose; they contrast beautifully in colour, texture and shape.

Filling the Gaps

Do your paving slabs look bare, your old stone paths have unsightly cracks? Bring them to life with some attractive plants that love to grow in gaps.

Do not despair if your paving is starting to crack and look shabby. Revitalize it with plants and turn it into a stunning garden feature.

If the cracks are not very large make them bigger with a cold chisel and hammer (don't be alarmed – it's really quite easy). Aim for cracks about 2.5-5cm/1-2in wide and deep enough to reach the soil below – 15cm/6in would be a good depth. Then fill the cracks with soil or compost such as John Innes No 2.

Going crazy
You may already have an area that is crazy paved – and this, of course, is ideal for planting. If the joins are filled with mortar that is cracking, break it up here and there, using a knife. Remove the broken pieces of mortar and fill the gaps with soil or compost.

These cracks and crevices can then become home to a wide range of colourful and interesting plants. Those that like well-drained or dry conditions are generally used and most are sun lovers.

You need not limit yourself to these plants, however, as there are also a few moisture-loving plants that are suitable (provided you can keep the soil or compost fairly damp). Also, there are several types of plants that enjoy being in light shade.

Dwarf plant types are generally best for filling gaps in paving. By far the majority of suitable plants are alpines or rock plants. Often they have an interesting habit of growth

and are mat or cushion forming. Some hardy perennials or small shrubs are also suitable.

Get rid of weeds
Before attempting to plant up a paved area it is vital to kill all perennial weeds. These thrive in cracks and crevices and are awkward to remove completely by hand. The only effective way to deal with stubborn weeds is to kill them at the roots which can be done by applying a weedkiller containing glyphosate, during the growing season.

Filling the cracks
You could use ordinary garden soil to fill the cracks prior to planting, provided it is not

An ordinary flight of steps is transformed by a glorious garland of campanula. Cunningly planted in the gap between the wall and the step this clever carpeter makes its way downstairs and crawls into the cracks.

heavy clay, but a soil-based potting compost would tend to produce better results. Whatever soil or compost you use, add one-third extra of horticultural grit to ensure it remains well aerated and drained.

The soil or compost must be pushed well into the cracks and crevices – in fact, to their extremities. Use a stick with a rounded end if necessary. The aim is to avoid an air pocket in the growing medium, otherwise plants will not root properly. Do not water the compost before planting, as it is much easier to fill cracks in paving if the soil is dry.

Choosing the plants
Choose plants that are small so you can fit them easily in to cracks and crevices. Many of the plants listed, especially the alpines, may be available in 8cm/3in pots.

When to grow
It is best to plant in early to mid spring although if conditions are mild and dryish early autumn is fine. If it is very cold or wet, or if you live in a chilly area it is better to stick to planting in spring.

If you buy plants in pots, carefully tease some of the soil away from the roots. On no account try to cram roots into the cracks – it is better to remove some more soil.

In a paved area, use a narrow-bladed trowel to dig a hole sufficiently deep to allow the roots to hang down to their

Old crazy paving in a well established garden (above left) has been given a new lease of life with these bright and cheerful plants. Thyme not only adds a dash of colour, it is also aromatic.

The chance meeting of these two flowers has produced such a harmonious effect against the severe rock background that they have been left to grow naturally.

If you tread the path to the garden seat (above), the wonderfully aromatic carpeters will release their perfumes.

This collection of plants (left) is ideal for filling cracks in paving. Bright yellow saxifrage partners well with snow-in-summer. The miniature rose adds a delicate touch.

The eye catching herringbone brick work (left) has been laid with gaps so that moss can easily self seed and spread to become part of the intricate design. The striking contrast of the green border draws out the mottled colours in the bricks themselves.

PLANT PROPAGATION

You can use small rooted divisions and offsets of your own plants or cuttings from friends' gardens. Many alpines and hardy perennials can be increased by division in spring. Offset-producing plants include *sempervivums*. Most shrubby plants can be propagated from cuttings. Allow the new roots to develop well before planting into paving.

full extent. If there is not enough room even for a narrow trowel, use a stick with a rounded end, then trickle fine soil around the roots and firm it in thoroughly.

Sowing seeds

Dwarf hardy and half-hardy annuals can also be grown from seed in between paving to provide summer colour.

It is a comparatively easy matter to sow seeds in the cracks, but do try to sow as thinly as possible to minimize thinning out of seedlings, then cover seeds lightly with fine soil or compost. Keep them well watered until the seeds have begun to sprout.

Hardy annuals may be sown during early or mid spring, but wait to sow half-hardy kinds until late spring when the danger of frost is past.

Easy maintenance

In the main, these dwarf plants are compact and need little in the way of tidying, except perhaps to remove dead flowers. Several spreading varieties are improved by being trimmed back lightly after flowering. This maintains a neat shape and encourages new growth.

Most of the plants in the list (overleaf) establish themselves quite rapidly. They soon make an attractive display, so giving a mature look to a newly paved area or fresh interest to tired old paving. Remember that the compost or soil in cracks and crevices will dry out rapidly during warm weather, so keep an eye on it and water as necessary. The best way to apply water is to use a garden sprinkler or a watering can with a fine rose.

An infusion of pink thrift with its mass of pretty flower heads (right) gives a lift to this dull, grey stone wall. Planted carefully in the crack between the rocks it grows diagonally up the slope retaining its soft cushion shape.

This beautiful bellflower (left) drapes elegantly over a rugged collection of rocks, softening the harsh edges and introducing colour as it grows. The romantic bluish-purple hues and exquisite star-shaped flowers make an eye-catching feature.

This sunny alyssum (below) is a happy resident of a wall, cascading beautifully over the edge. The multitude of bright yellow pompon flower heads will give bright colour in springtime.

P ROJECT   PLANTING IN PAVING

Plan ahead by getting rid of weeds (it is better to use a weedkiller as it is difficult to make sure you have removed all the roots by hand). Find out the mature size of your plants in order to work out planting distances. Here, saxifrages, campanulas and sempervivums have been chosen to provide a succession of flowers from spring until late summer. Alyssum can be grown from seed and so it is easy to sow in crevices; it will also self seed in following seasons. Unlike camomile and thyme which, when stepped on, give off an aroma, these plants should not be planted where people are likely to tread.

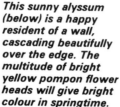

1 Make a space larger than plant' roots. Add a little compost, insert plant, fill hole with more compost.

GOOD GAP FILLERS

BLUES

Bellflower: summer, spreading habit.
Globularia *(G. cordifolia)*: summer, mat-forming habit.
Violet cress: blue-tinged flowers, summer annual.
Baby blue eyes: blue and white, summer, hardy annual.
Horned violet: spring-summer, spreading clumps.

FOLIAGE

Corsican mint: tiny aromatic leaves, creeping.
Stonecrop: fleshy grey purplish rosettes, mat-forming.
Cobweb houseleek: webbed rosettes.

MULTI-COLOURED

Livingstone daisy: summer, half-hardy annual.
Sun plant *(Portulaca grandiflora)*: summer, half-hardy annual.

PINKS AND REDS

New Zealand burr: spiny red seed heads, mat-forming habit.
Stone cress *(Aethionema)*:'Warley Rose', pink flowers,
   spring-summer, compact.
Thrift: pink flowers, late spring, cushion-forming.
Maiden pink: summer, mat-forming habit.
Alpine fleabane, summer, clump-forming.
Stork's bill: summer, hummock-forming.
Cranesbill *(Geranium dalmaticum)*: summer, prostrate.
Baby's breath *(Gypsophila repens)*: white or pink flowers, summer,
   prostrate.

This small, spreading alpine saxifrage (left), flowers in early spring. The unusual spiky clump formed by this species, S. × apiculata, is refined by the simple, graceful, yellow flowers.

This attractive bright pink thyme (right) has hundreds of tiny flowers which are beautifully scented and are particularly attractive to bees. This common variety is called Thymus serpyllum.

2 Making sure all weeds have been removed, fill cracks with compost and sow seeds sparingly.

3 Carefully add a thin layer of grit round the base of plants and over seeds. Water seeds regularly.

Virginian stock: pink, white or red, self sows freely, hardy annual.
Primula 'Wanda': crimson-purple flowers, spring, clump-forming.
Soapwort: pink flowers, summer, mat-forming.
Moss campion (Saponaria ocymoides): spring, hummock-forming.
Thyme (T. lanuginosus): summer, aromatic foliage, mat-forming.

YELLOWS

Yarrow: yellow flowers, summer, mat-forming.
Alyssum (A. montanum): yellow flowers, early spring prostrate habit.
Broom (Cytisus ardoinii): late spring, hummock-forming.
Alpine wallflowers: late spring, bushy habit.
St. John's wort (Hypericum olympicum): yellow flowers, summer, bushy.
Poached-egg flower: white and yellow flowers, summer, hardy annual.
Morisia monanthos: late spring-early summer, prostrate rosettes.
Cinquefoil (Potentilla x tonguei): summer, mat-forming.
Saxifrage x apiculata: light yellow flowers, early spring, cushion-forming habit.
Thyme (T. praecox): tiny aromatic leaves, prostrate.

WHITES

Maiden pink: summer, mat-forming habit.
Mountain avens: late spring, mat-forming.
Stork's bill: summer, hummock-forming.
Baby's breath (Gypsophila repens): summer, prostrate.
Chamois cress (Hutchinsia alpina): late spring-summer, tufted habit.
Candytuft (Iberis saxatilis): spring-early summer, bushy.
Edelweiss: white flowers surrounded by grey bracts, spring, tufted.
Horned violet: spring-summer, spreading.

Raising their cheerful faces to the sun, these Livingstone daisies (above) are well adapted to growing in the smallest of cracks and crevices. They grow to 15cm/6in high and have a spreading habit which enables them to grow over rugged terrain.

A slightly taller addition to the gaps in your paving could be these modern pinks. They grow to 37cm/15in and are faster growing than their relatives in the dianthus family. In very mild weather they may flower right up until mid-winter.

A Courtyard Garden

At first glance, a city garden or yard can be a dreary prospect, but with a touch of imagination you can transform it into a glorious garden.

it was possible to create oases of lush vegetation at the very heart of the most densely populated of cities.

Although, at first sight, a concreted basement area or a weed-choked yard surrounded by blank walls does not look too promising, a lick of light paint, the right paving materials and some carefully selected plants can transform it into a living treasure, chock full of delights.

Not only will such a garden provide a small haven of peace in the middle of the hustle and bustle of city life, but also something the city's horizons do not always offer – a pleasant view from the window.

Making plans
Planning is always important in creating a garden; much more so when gardening on a

Simplicity is the keynote in planning a courtyard garden (above). Here, lush foliage plants create shade on an otherwise undistinguished wall, while tables and chairs for outdoor eating sit on a paved patio, which is edged with easy-maintenance container plants.

Most towns and cities are a hotch-potch of houses, flats, office buildings, shops and industrial estates that have grown up over centuries without any recognizable overall plan or scheme.

This haphazard growth took place without reference to the needs of the gardener. Inner city land is a rare and expensive commodity, and city gardens tend to be small and oddly shaped, having been crammed into left-over nooks

and crannies between building developments. Surrounding high-rise buildings may severely restrict sunlight.

A room with a view
Up until the 1950s, this lack of garden space did not matter so much, as few people even tried to grow anything in the heavily polluted atmosphere of old city centres. The Clean Air Act changed all that.

After the smog cleared, people slowly came to realize that

REFLECTED GLORY

Brighten up a dull corner by fixing a large mirror to the wall. Disguise and soften the edges by framing it with trellis and growing climbers up it. Ivy and some honeysuckle will tolerate shade and are evergreen for winter interest.

The mirror will reflect precious light and will also give a sense of space as it reflects the glories of your garden.

To increase the sensation of space, put handsome pots filled with hostas and other interesting foliage plants along the sides of a path leading up to the mirror.

BRIGHT IDEAS

There is an air of tranquillity in this courtyard garden (left), with its predominantly white and green colour scheme. In time, climbing plants will provide the necessary boundary from its neighbour.

A water feature (right) adds a touch of class to any garden. Nowadays, a small fountain is not particularly expensive or difficult to install; many come with their own pumping systems and do not involve major re-plumbing.

The shelter of a sunny courtyard wall suits the tender Passiflora caerulea (below), which is notable for its white and blue- or purple-banded flowers, but which can also produce egg-shaped, fleshy, edible fruits in autumn.

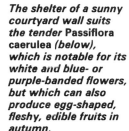

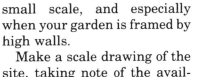

small scale, and especially when your garden is framed by high walls.

Make a scale drawing of the site, taking note of the available light. Is the garden shaded by neighbouring trees and buildings? Does it have a summer suntrap?

If you make several photocopies of your basic plan and mark the areas in shade at different times of the day, you will have a better idea where to put things. Light and shade will not only determine what you plant and where, but also where you locate garden features; you do not want to build a barbecue in the only sunny corner, for example.

If there is a general lack of light, paint the boundary walls a light colour to a height of around 1.8m/6ft. This will reflect light back into your garden as well as giving a bright and airy atmosphere to a previously gloomy yard. Though white reflects best, pastel colours may better complement your planting scheme.

Cutting down

Having drawn a plan of the site, it is time to think about what you want from it. Make a list of everything you can think of that you and your fa-

mily would like. Inevitably, there will be far too much for the space available.

If you find it difficult to visualize the end result, cut out shapes to represent raised beds, a water feature, a seating area and so on, and place them on your plan.

This enables you to shift

THE EYE OF THE BEHOLDER

Changes of level are important in a town garden. They enhance the feeling of privacy by keeping the eye of the visitor firmly in the garden and not on its surroundings.

This desirable effect may be achieved with steps, raised beds, climbing plants and structures like an arbour. Raising particularly handsome pots or statues on plinths helps too. Hanging baskets, climbers and decorative wall-planters all encourage the viewer to keep within the garden's boundaries.

things about and decide which design is most pleasing. It will also help you to decide what must go. A general rule of thumb in designing a small garden is that less is better.

Hard choices

Once you have decided on the overall design of your garden you must make some decisions on what materials to use for permanent fixtures like raised beds and paving.

The choice you make for paving depends largely on how big your yard is. If the area is small, then the more expensive options such as tiles, stone slabs or bricks are attractively affordable; prefabricated squares of wooden decking make a cheaper, practical alternative. In a shady yard, use light-coloured materials.

Once you have the structure of your garden settled, you can begin to colour in the rough outline with plants.

Choosing plants

An unexpected bonus of gardening in the heart of a city is that conditions are more sheltered and the heat from sur-

CLIMBERS FOR SHADE

Clematis alpina or *C. macropetala* types do well in shady gardens and are hardy. They have small, bell-shaped flowers.

Members of the ivy family are invaluable for difficult conditions.

Hydrangea petiolaris (also known as *H. anomala petiolaris*) has lacy white flowers in summer and will tolerate fairly damp, shady conditions.

Various honeysuckles will perfume a shady garden. A notable example is the attractive climber *L. japonica*, which is fragrant and evergreen.

Winter-flowering jasmine (*Jasminum nudiflorum*) has small, yellow flowers i—n late winter or early spring, while white summer jasmine (*J. officinale*) bears fragrant white flowers in late summer and autumn.

rounding buildings keeps the temperature a few degrees higher than it is in the suburbs or in the country.

This widens your choice of plants, as you can afford to risk over-wintering tender subjects. *Passiflora caerulea*, for instance, is a lovely climber that will tolerate winter city temperatures. It can grow to a height of 10m/30ft and can look wonderful against a sun-

ny wall. It is fast growing and has the advantage of being semi-evergreen, thus providing winter interest.

Small, enclosed spaces need some variation in height to be interesting, so it is important not to restrict your planting to ground level. Climbers and hanging baskets are essential ingredients of a creative planting scheme, giving the necessary height and relieving the

This striking, rather formal, courtyard garden (above) relies entirely on foliage plants for its effect. Variegated hostas provide ground cover interest against the background wall, supported by plants of different shapes and textures. The raised beds rely on a similar assortment of feathery shapes and textures.

GARDEN NOTES

relieving the monotony of the surrounding walls.

Containers are an important element in a courtyard garden. What you plant in them depends on your taste and prevailing conditions. Petunias are always good value,

as are antirrhinums, lobelias and pansies.

A sunny, enclosed yard is ideal for a delightful scented garden. Herbs will provide a heady scent in a warm, enclosed space. Rosemary, thyme and sage are hardy and fra-

In a city garden (above), container-grown herbs can be both useful and decorative. Chives, caraway and sage are among those grown here.

Mixed ceramic and earthenware containers (left) can make a bold statement in a gloomy courtyard corner.

The pretty, bell-shaped flowers of Clematis alpina 'Frances Rivis' (below) look lovely trained on a trellis or wall. The plant will do well on exposed north-facing walls.

grant. Lavender is always a good plant to have; its silvery leaves bring interest in winter and act as a lovely foil for bright summer bedding, while its headily aromatic leaves and flowers make a delightful bonus both for you and for any bees that may pass by.

Some climbers, like clematis, enjoy having their roots in shade and their heads in the sun. An arbour can provide them with these conditions. Climbing roses will give an arbour a romantic appeal. Overhead beams will supply a stout frame for climbing or rambling roses and you can hang baskets from them for extra flowering interest.

City life can be stressful and one of nature's best tranquillizers is the tinkling sound of running water. There are many ways to achieve this in a small garden. A wall mounted fountain is best when ground space is at a premium. Many designs are now available and it will pay you to shop around before buying. It is best to save this purchase until you have decided on things like paving so that you can choose one that blends in well with the rest of the garden design.

Precisely because a courtyard is small, it lends itself to night lighting. A few spotlights will help you to enjoy your garden from the inside in the evening, as well as providing added security.

Shade-lovers suitable for containers include the lovely camellia family; be sure to provide acid soil for these. Cyclamen, scilla and some of the fritillaries are among the bulbs that thrive in shade.

Fuchsias look stunning in containers and those with a trailing habit are excellent subjects for hanging baskets. Some are frost hardy and some are not, but in such a sheltered spot even the less hardy types may survive the winter. You can always bring them into the house in very severe weather. Standard fuchsias look really lovely in a formal courtyard garden but should be overwintered indoors.

Peace and privacy

Privacy is hard to come by in a city; your space will probably be overlooked by surrounding buildings. An arbour can solve this problem for you, while also adding much-needed height to your garden.

A simple arch, or some beams fixed across the corner of the yard, can provide not only a seating area sheltered from casual observation, but a support for climbers.

Imaginative use of an old fire grate (left) adds interest to this densely planted and colourful corner.

Vertical or horizontal beams (below left) provide not only privacy but a support for climbing plants or hanging baskets. Here, ground-level planting of containers with such summer favourites as fuchsias, busy Lizzies and geraniums adds a mass of cheerful blooms.

The water from this unusual jug 'fountain' (right) supports the dense, green foliage of the moisture-loving Soleirolia soleirolii and also the impressive arum lily (Zantedeschia aethiopica), a marginal water plant.

The elegant Tulipa 'Queen of the Night' with T. 'Athleet' (below) help to create a peaceful, quiet spot in the garden.

A TOUCH OF THE SUN

A city yard can be transformed into a Mediterranean garden.

Cap the surrounding walls with old-fashioned, terracotta roofing tiles. Paint the walls white, and carefully place brackets for hanging baskets and ornamental wall planters where they will catch the sun. Make sure to leave wall space for climbing plants.

Splash out on some good outdoor tiles for paving; bright designs suit a shaded garden while terracotta coloured ones look good in a sunnier site.

Install a wall mounted water-feature with a classical theme or a small central fountain to enhance the Mediterranean mood.

Select plenty of pelargoniums for pots on window-sills, steps and raised areas. Choose ferns and ivies for shaded areas.

An Outdoor Room

A paved patio bridges the gap between house and garden. The right plants create a sheltered and pretty space to entertain, relax or eat outdoors.

A patio can be the most lived-in place in the garden. In fine weather, when house and garden chores are done, a period of relaxation on a patio surrounded by fragrance, colourful blooms and the hum of insects is one of the gardener's rewards.

But, before you relax, you may have to make decisions and carry out some creative planting to decorate what is essentially an outdoor 'room'. It is an unusual room, though. There is likely to be only one high wall, no roof and a paved floor!

By using plants, trellis and pergola you can 'fill out' the room, adding height, screens and shelter, and create a decorative scheme in any of a range of styles. The right planting scheme can create an intimate, sheltered area that you will be able to enjoy over many years.

When you sit down to enjoy your patio, you do not want to be faced with weeding and fussing over plants, but you do want pleasant colour, fragrance and ornament.

Trees for the patio

Whatever its size, your patio will look interesting if it has a mixture of permanent background plants, including evergreen and deciduous trees and shrubs and some medium-height perennials and annuals to clothe the lower margins near ground level. Plants in movable containers provide good splashes of annual colour, while window boxes and hanging baskets offer interest at different levels.

There are several trees

which can be grown in large wooden or terracotta tubs to provide you with dappled shade and screening from your neighbours' gaze.

Silver birch (*Betula pendula*) and robinia offer fresh young leaves in spring and good stem colour. They are also upright in their growth, so won't shade the patio undu-

ly. When they are kept in large tubs, their growth is restricted to around 3m/10ft.

Specially trained standard trees and shrubs with bushy or weeping tops are popular as their scale is appropriate for small-space growing.

Many soft and top fruit trees are available for patio cultivation. Not only will they provide

A well-planted patio and the right furniture can bring the garden into the home and the home into the garden. This rule applies whether the patio is a warm sun-trap or a cooler, more shaded area (above).

Climbing roses make excellent patio plants, clothing a trellis or a wall with foliage and flowers. Rosa 'New Dawn' (right) is a particularly good choice, as its handsome, pale-pink double blooms fill the air with a sweetly evocative perfume.

A bed planted with nepeta, which has a trailing habit, will soften the edge of a patio (right above); here, its mauve flowers contrast with a golden-yellow lily. A bed is not strictly necessary, however; a fine floral display can be achieved using containers and hanging baskets (right).

height and spring flowers, but in summer or autumn you will have a patio-grown harvest. Best choices include the single stem Ballerina apple trees. A row of these planted in suitable containers will provide a perfect summer screen.

Up the wall

Climbing plants such as roses, wisteria and clematis will provide vertical cover, softening the harsh edges of the back wall, and, with the help of trellis or other supports, will provide parts of the missing 'walls'. Variegated ivies such

CONTAINER CARE

GROWING TIPS

Plants in containers or restricted conditions will not grow as large or tall as they would if free-standing, but they will need regular watering, feeding and dead-heading or pruning during the growing season.

MAINTAINING TRELLIS

For easy wall maintenance, fix sections of trellis to strong, treated wooden battens. Hang the whole trellis on small hooks or nails. When the wall needs painting or pointing it is easy to remove the trellis and its plant.

as 'Goldheart' and 'Buttercup' will cling closely to the brick-work, bringing interesting and sunny leaf colour that is welcome all through the year.

For evergreen shrub cover choose *Garrya elliptica*. It grows fairly tall and, as it does so, seems to flatten itself against a wall. In winter it produces lovely soft green catkins that trail from its branches, adding to the grace of its upward sweep.

A patio canopy

Trailing and climbing plants offer possibilities as 'roofing' materials to drape across pergolas and provide dappled shade and shelter for those sitting on the patio.

Honeysuckle, vigorous roses such as *R. filipes* 'Kiftsgate' and climbers such as Russian vine (*Polygonum baldschuanicum*), will quickly grow up pillars and scramble across the patio canopy. Russian vine is such a vigorous plant that unless it is kept sternly in check, it may soon block out all light, thereby defeating the object of partial shade.

Floral carpets

Ground cover plants such as sedums, saxifrages and creeping thymes will grow happily between the pavers. In garden beds next to the patio, choose mounding plants such as lady's mantle (*Alchemilla mollis*) and nepeta to trail over the patio edge and soften the hard paving edges.

To create an informal style remove a few pavers at random and use the space to grow alyssum, lavender and even chamomile.

Before planting you may need to remove hardcore and sand. Work in some organic matter and water well before setting in the plants.

ROOF-TOP GARDENS

If your patio is on a roof top, keep weight to a minimum by using light-weight containers such as plastic and glass fibre. Use peat-based composts to further reduce the load, but do not allow them to dry out, as they are difficult to remoisten.

Keep pots away from the centre of the roof-top patio.

Patio gardening is not just about flowers. Fruits and herbs can also be grown (above left); here, Ballerina apple trees and tall tomatoes are underplanted with parsley and chives.

A sheltered, sunny patio is an ideal spot for a formal pond (right); if it is not built in, a water feature can be created by lifting a paver or two and digging out the soil below. If your patio (and barbecue), is in a shady corner, pleasing effects can be created using potted ferns, which flourish in such an environment (above centre).

A patio overflowering with Nicotiana (above right) will provide a fragrant atmosphere in which to eat on summer evenings.

You may wish to keep plants to a minimum, preferring the structural work of the patio to show through. In such a scheme you can use shapely plants as architectural focal points to complement the colour and textures of the brickwork and paving. New Zealand flax (*Phormium tenax*) is one such plant. It's full of drama, with large, strap-shaped leaves fanning out into a showy head. Set in a terracotta urn, it will make a strong and eye-catching focal point.

Focus on fragrance

Scented plants such as tobacco (*Nicotiana spp.*) and clove pink will provide pools of fragrance for you to enjoy as you eat, sit and relax in this delightful outdoor garden room.

Roses such as 'New Dawn',

BARBECUE HERBS

DON'T FORGET!

If you plan to cook on the patio it's essential to have a herb bed or container close at hand. Use rosemary and thyme in your marinades. Cut handfuls of aromatic twigs from them to throw onto the hot coals to provide aromatic, smoky flavours.

summer flowering jasmine (*Jasminum polyanthum*), Christmas box (*Sarcococca confusa*) and the compact mock orange (*Philadelphus microphyllus*) will all offer strong, pleasing perfumes at different seasons of the year.

Many plants, such as butterfly bushes (*Buddleia davi-*

dii), attract butterflies to sip their nectar. Herb plants such as thyme are great bee attractants and the poached egg plant (*Limnanthes douglassi*) attracts the benign hoverflies that keep down aphid populations. A bird bath or small water feature on the patio may attract birds, but your own presence is a deterrent.

Patio containers

If your patio is on the same level as the rest of the garden it can be fringed by herbaceous borders that spill over it, softening its lines. Here you will have no extra maintenance problems as there is no real division between patio and garden.

If the patio is on a different level you will have to use containers to grow many of the plants around its edges. Go for the biggest containers you can afford, as they require less maintenance. Larger containers retain water better, and there is less need to repot annually. Using larger containers you can be more creative and imaginative in your patio planting plans.

Terracotta, plastic and wood are the most popular materials for containers and they are available at garden centres in a wide range of styles.

A splash of colour

Hanging baskets and window boxes fixed to the house wall are ideal for providing splashes of colour at different heights. Place them where you can water them easily and add water-retaining polymer granules to the compost. Use special container composts that include controlled release fertilizers. This ensures that nutrients do not wash away when you water.

Raised beds

Purpose built raised beds or beds set into low brick walls are ideal permanent containers for patio plants.

When constructing a raised bed, leave small weep-holes in the brick work, to drain off excess water. Before you plant up add a thick layer of drain-

Furniture can set the tone for patio planting. The light, lacy lines of a wrought-iron bench can combine with white-washed walls, painted shutters and clouds of trailing, small-flowered plants to create a sunny, almost Mediterranean look (left), while rustic wooden furniture is better suited by more substantial, low-growing plants that make masses of solid colour, like begonias and fuchsias (above).

PROJECT

A PEBBLE BED

Individually potted plants on a patio often look untidy and it is difficult to keep them well watered in drought conditions. Both problems can be solved by making a pebble bed.

Group the plants to make an attractive display. Scatter pea shingle or washed gravel in and around the pot bases until you have a 5-7cm/2-3in layer. Edge the shingle bed with larger stones and water well. Wet the gravel thoroughly.

The gravel acts as a mulch; the water around it evaporates at a slower rate, raising the humidity around the plants.

age material to the base. Fill the bed with a good, organically enriched loamy soil.

Raised beds are ideal for alpines. If you plan to use them instead for camellias, rhododendrons, ericas or other lime-hating plants add an ericaceous compost.

Outdoor furniture

Once the planting is done, it's time to sit or lie back, relax, and enjoy the fruits of your labours. Your choice of garden seats and loungers will depend on the size of the patio and your budget.

Garden furniture comes in all shapes and sizes and can be

made from wood, plastic, wrought iron and tubular metal. Weight, strength, weather-resistance, style and comfort will all be factors behind your choice.

Cast or wrought iron furniture is heavy and weather resistant, but may show surface rusting after a time. It may also break if knocked onto a hard surface. However, its permanence makes it easier to integrate in an overall scheme. Aluminium deck chairs and loungers are much lighter and cheaper but are best kept out of wet weather.

Wooden furniture looks good and will last for many years given good treatment and regular preservative care with a linseed or colour-based oil. It's always preferable if you can store it indoors in winter or at least cover it up.

Lightweight furniture

Plastic deck chairs and tables are the lightest and most weather resistant choice, but for extra comfort you will need soft cushions. Most garden centres sell a wide range of outdoor furniture complete with high fashion upholstered cushions and padded lounger covers.

Ultimate relaxation and comfort is hammock-shaped. If there are trees growing in the ground near the patio, suspend the hammock from them. Free-standing hammocks supported by their own frame are also available in a range of colours and fit relaxingly into a patio furnishing scheme.

SHORT CUTS

TIME RELEASE COMPOSTS

In hanging baskets and other patio containers use composts with controlled-release fertilizers. When you water, the nutrients will not wash away if the basket or container overflows.

Patio containers can feature either a specimen plant or a mixed group. A dramatic example of the former is Phormium tenax, which grows to 3m/10ft and has several coloured or variegated varieties (above left). When planting a mixed container (above), the plants' growing habits and the colour and texture of their flowers and foliage must all be taken into account. Here, the fresh greens and orange hues of nasturtiums are set off by the silver-grey foliage of helichrysum and underpinned by the creeping leaves of Ajuga reptans.

Outdoor Entertaining

With a little planning and minimal expense, even the smallest garden can be turned into an ideal setting for summer barbecues, lunches, teas and dinner parties.

One of the great joys of having a garden is being able to use it as an outdoor 'room' for entertaining friends. There is nothing to beat idling away a warm summer evening nibbling a barbecued chicken wing or two, enjoying a drink and breathing in the mingled scents of flowers and charcoal-grilled food.

Being outdoors gives an occasion a much more informal, relaxed feel, and helps people to enjoy themselves. A daytime or evening barbecue is the most popular event, whether it takes the form of a party with snacks cooked outdoors, or a more serious meal prepared on the barbecue and eaten at a table. Sunday lunch can also taste extra special if eaten *al fresco*, and children always love to have tea picnic-style on the lawn.

Patio planning

If you give dinner parties, holding them outdoors – or perhaps starting outdoors, then moving back in as the temperature drops and the serious eating begins – makes a refreshing change, and is a particularly good icebreaker if your guests do not know each other very well.

If you plan to invite more than a handful of people, it is best to hold the event on a patio. Lots of feet trampling over your lawn for several hours will do it no good at all, especially if the soil is less than bone dry.

Building a patio, or enlarging an existing one, is quite a simple job, as there is no need to lay a foundation of rubble – just lay slabs on a bed of sand about 5cm/2in thick. Garden and DIY centres or builder's merchants usually stock a wide choice of concrete paving slabs in all sizes, shapes and colours – choose small-sized ones for ease of laying.

If the ground has to be dug over first, leave it to settle before laying the slabs, then firm it by laying down planks and walking over them.

What could be more pleasant than entertaining guests in this setting. The circular table and patio (above), framed by an abundance of shrubs and flowers, form an almost self-contained garden 'room'.

Barbecues can be bought in all shapes and sizes, but it is easy to build a permanent one of bricks and building slabs (above right) that will double as a stand for pots.

Add a touch of fragrance to the garden when the sun goes down with night-scented flowers such as the tobacco plant, Nicotiana alata (right).

46

When a patio is put next to a house wall, it must be at least 15cm/6in below the damp-proof course, and slope gently away to carry off rainwater. Make sure the finished level matches up with any existing paving or adjacent grass, as even small changes of level can be dangerous.

Make a patio as large as you can, in relation to the size of the garden, not only to give people plenty of room, but so that you can site the barbecue where it will not cause any annoyance to neighbours.

Barbecue choice

A permanent barbecue, built of bricks and paving slabs with a metal grill to hold the food, is easy to build, and makes a garden feature which can be used as a stand for plants in pots when not in use. Site it away from the house, trees, shrubs, fences and timber buildings. Portable barbecues are generally more popular in small gardens, as they can be put away when not needed, and also sited to suit the wind direction.

Most of today's barbecues are designed to burn charcoal

or cook some of the food indoors, perhaps in a microwave.

Cooking food for any number of people on a barbecue takes quite some time, so it needs to be at a convenient working height to avoid backache. If you are tall, a hibachi-type barbecue mounted on a table is probably a better bet than a free-standing one, as these are often rather low. Do not forget to provide somewhere to put the food and plates. Using the ground is inconvenient and can be dangerous in the dark.

Outdoor meals

Even if you do not have a barbecue – or if the weather seems too uncertain to risk outdoor cooking – you can still entertain barbecue-style by cooking hamburgers, chicken portions, pork spare ribs, baked potatoes and corn on the cob in the kitchen for guests to take outdoors. Hot soup is a good starter if the

chips or briquettes, and range from the simple hibachi type, ideal for grilling a few hamburgers, to elaborate free-standing affairs on wheels incorporating windshields, warming ovens and machinery for spit-roasting chickens and turning kebabs. For a small one-off barbecue you can even buy disposable barbecue kits.

If you plan to do lots of entertaining and want trouble-free cooking, you can purchase expensive gas-fired barbecues that work off a gas cylinder or connect to the house gas supply, or even electric models that plug into the mains. The burners heat reusable volcanic rock that gives the food a similar smoky flavour to that created by charcoal.

Choose your barbecue according to the number of people to be catered for. An area of about 45cm/18in across provides enough space to cook food for eight people. For a bigger party you will need to buy or borrow a second barbecue,

evening is a bit chilly – serve it in mugs rather than bowls.

Outdoor meals do not have to be barbecues, it is perfectly possible to hold a formal dinner party in the garden, but be careful to have a fall-back plan, just in case it rains.

When laying the table, bear in mind that there is often a light breeze around just waiting to snatch things away. Do not use a tablecloth, or secure it to the table with drawing pins; anchor napkins under plates and avoid tall vases of flowers. Use insect-repellent candles as table decorations.

Plan the menu with care, as it is easy for plates of food to cool off rapidly in the open air. A good choice is a cold starter, followed by a rich peasant-style casserole served straight from the oven on hot plates, with baked potatoes, and an ice cream-based dessert.

Furniture

For a barbecue you will not need much extra garden furniture, as people will happily eat standing up, and you need to leave plenty of room for them to circulate. A more formal meal, however, needs some kind of proper table. In a good-sized garden, a permanent timber picnic table – the kind with attached benches – is ideal but for small ones it is better to use folding or stackable tables that can be stored away.

A spectacular cluster of strongly-scented honeysuckle, (Lonicera × americana,) has been attractively placed in a container (above) to make a striking cornerpiece to a patio.

Highlight the garden by hanging lanterns (above left) from trees above the eating area at an evening barbecue. Not only do they lend a romantic glow to the proceedings, but their light allows guests to more easily pick and choose their food.

Train perfumed jasmine up walls (left) to provide a cool green contrast to red bricks. It can also be successfully grown on pergolas, arches and fences.

Relax and unwind with a delicious lunch (right) in the open air, but on summer days always ensure that there is plenty of shade when the sun is at its hottest.

IMPROVISATIONS

- Make a dining table by covering a wallpaper-pasting table with a plastic cloth. Or use a flush door set on trestles.
- Provide extra seating by bringing out sofa cushions and laying against a wall.
- Use a portable sawhorse-cum-vice as a stand for a hibachi-type barbecue.
- Use upturned plastic crates as side tables, and as seats if they are strong enough.

BRIGHT IDEAS

49

Do not use your dining table, if it rains you will have to struggle to get it back in before it is ruined. Dining or kitchen chairs can be useful, but keep them on hard surfaces – on lawns they can cause accidents, if one leg suddenly sinks, and pit the lawn.

If the party starts in the middle of the day, when the sun is at its hottest, provide plenty of shade, otherwise people may get sunstroke without noticing until it is too late! Put tables and chairs in shady spots or provide tables with central umbrellas.

Lighting

For an evening party, there is nothing like garden lighting to add a touch of glamour and excitement – it can also serve a practical purpose as strangers will not be able to find their way safely in the dark.

It is quite easy to rig up a string of fairy lights, supporting them on fences and shrubs, or hanging them in a tree, and plugging them into a cable reel leading back into the house. For safety, buy an RCD (Residual Current Device) which breaks the circuit quickly should the cable be damaged. If you have camping lanterns or oil lamps, press them into service. Candles constantly blow out, and are a bit of a fire risk, unless you enclose them in glass. To illuminate key areas, say, around the barbecue or a flight of steps, buy one or two garden flares that you can stick in the ground.

If you give many evening barbecues the easiest way to install permanent outdoor lighting is to buy a lighting kit that connects up to a low-voltage transformer. This is hidden in the garage or indoors and connected to a power socket. A low-voltage cable runs from the transformer to light fittings mounted on spikes for sticking in the ground. This can safely be left running along the surface, but inspect it regularly to keep it out of the way. You can also make good use of the house lights by keeping the curtains open.

The evening primrose (Oenothera sp.) gives off a faint scent (above), but its profuse, bright yellow flowers have the unusual habit of opening wide at night, thereby enhancing the garden after dark.

Choose garden furniture that harmonizes with the rest of the surroundings (left). Here, the addition of a tablecloth and umbrella that echo the green of the outbuilding's shutters and door give this patio a fresh, cool look.

Miniature Gardens

Short of space? By using compact plants, you can create an entire landscape in miniature. Perfect for an interesting feature or, in a tiny plot, a whole garden.

This miniature railway has been lovingly set in a miniature landscape at Babbacombe Model Village in Devon. The railway itself and the model people are perfectly in scale with a hillside 'wood', tiny golf course and parkland. Much of the effect is achieved by trimming tiny shrubs into the shapes of mature trees.

Enthusiasts have created miniature landscapes for nearly two centuries. The Victorians made rockeries that were virtually scale models of parts of the Alps, correct in every detail right down to the lookout points and telescopes. The creators of miniature villages, like the famous one in the English Cotswolds, surrounded their tiny houses with gardens on the same scale, for authenticity. And garden railway fans have for many years built, not only scale-model track layouts running round their gardens, but also very detailed miniature landscapes to 'naturalize' them.

Nowadays, many gardeners are turning to miniaturized gardens both to keep up with fashions, and to make the best use of space.

Changing trends

In large gardens, the current trend is away from wide open vistas, and increasingly towards dividing the space up into smaller, more intimate, 'gardens within gardens'. One of these could well be a miniature garden. If you are a compulsive designer, you could create a series of miniature gardens within a large plot.

But in a pocket handkerchief-sized space, you can turn the whole area into a miniature garden – the style is tailor-made for it. By using lots of fine detail, you can enjoy watching an ever-changing pattern of plants unfold in front of your windows all year.

Proportion and scale

Even though you probably do not want to create a true 'scale model' garden, it is important to keep an eye on the proportions if you want your miniature landscape to look right.

The smaller the space, the smaller the plants you will need. But it is also important to choose plants that are in proportion to each other. It is no good, for instance, mixing shrubs that are simply compact with those that are positively miniature – they just will not go well together. So decide early on which you want, and check ultimate plant heights and spreads when you buy.

Choosing plants

Anybody can create a small garden from small plants. But if you are making a real miniature garden, the trick lies in finding plants that give the same effect as a full-sized plant, but on a smaller scale. There are miniature versions of many popular garden plants – think of dwarf rhododendrons and conifers, miniature narcissi and roses, edging box, and so on, which are found in most garden centres. (As a rough guide, anything with a latin name ending in the word *nana* or *pygmea* will be a small version of the original plant).

There are also a good many flowers that are specially bred to be compact versions of tra-

- In designing your miniature garden, follow the same guidelines as for planning a normal garden, but using smaller plants chosen to provide the same sort of effects — eg seasonal colour, variation in plant shape and height, contrasts of texture and so on.
- Don't try to be too clever with the design. The result should be instantly recognizable as a complete garden in miniature. But unlike a conventional garden which is usually seen from one direction, remember a miniature garden will be viewed from above as well.
- Keep everything in the garden to a similar scale. Avoid mixing ultra dwarf varieties with those that are merely compact, or the result will look odd.
- Take trouble over detail. It is fun hunting out 'scaled down' accessories like containers, ornaments and even gravel (try the sort sold for fish tanks) to complete the scene.
- Don't try to miniaturize full-sized trees, shrubs and roses by cutting them back hard — they won't flower, and instead produce thickets of vigorous suckers.
- Try to avoid having a lawn; they never really look in scale. If necessary, go for a 'lawn' of pearlwort or moss (which need well compacted soil and moist, slightly shaded conditions), or the dwarf creeping thyme (*Thymus serphyllum* 'Minimus') in a sunny dryish spot. Or you could use fine (ryegrass-free) lawn seed and keep the grass cut very closely.

ditionally tall plants, such as many newer varieties of sunflowers, delphiniums, asters, and other flowers which are often only one-third normal height. (You can grow from seed, though many compact perennials can be had from mail order plant catalogues).

In a very restricted space, even dwarf versions of 'normal' plants can be too big, so in some circumstances you may need to cheat a bit. Many rock plants, for instance, can be

Low-growing plants (above), especially those that form clumps and can be trimmed into desired shapes, are invaluable in a mini landscape. They can be shaped to resemble trees or bushes, and flowering species can look like beds of full-sized annuals. The plants here are a dwarf conifer, thymes, Dianthus, violas, saxifrage and sempervivum.

If you are new to garden design and do not feel confident of creating a pretty garden at the first attempt, do not plant your miniature garden straight away. Since the plants are naturally small, they should be quite happy left in pots for the first year. Instead, simply 'plunge' them, pot and all, into prepared ground. That way, you can easily lift and reposition plants until you are quite happy with the layout, before planting them properly. In the same way, any new plants you are adding to the garden can be 'plunged' temporarily while you decide where they look best. Try two or three different places, leaving the plant for a week or so in each one, while you make up your mind.

Geranium dalmaticum (right) is a tiny geranium often used in rockeries. It grows to a height of 8-10cm/3-4in and is evergreen except in the harshest winters. It can be used in any situation where larger geraniums would grow.

SHORT CUTS

used to replace traditional herbaceous garden flowers in a miniature landscape, provided the drainage is good. Visit the rock garden section of the garden centre to find small species of pinks, artemisia and campanula, for example.

Micro-mini plants

If you are prepared to hunt them out, you can also find very unusual 'micro-miniature' species of trees and shrubs, including things like willow, birch and rowan which only grow a foot or so high.

These can be useful in very small-scale gardens, given good drainage, or in alpine gardens. These are mostly available from rock plant specialists; you can find suppliers

UNUSUAL MICRO-MINI TREES AND SHRUBS		
Betula nana 'Glengarry'	tiny twiggy birch tree	25cm/10in
Cryptomeria japonica 'Vilmoriniana'	bushy red Japanese conifer	30cm/1ft
Cytisus ardoinii 'Cottage'	cream-flowered broom	40cm/16in
Forsythia viridissima 'Bronxensis'	dwarf forsythia	30cm/1ft
Hypericum olympicum	tiny version of rose of Sharon	20cm/8in
Salix 'Boydii'	gnarled upright alpine willow	25cm/10in
Salix lanata 'Stuartii'	small willow with yellow catkins	50cm/20in
Sorbus reducta	tiny gnarled rowan, red berries, autumn tints	40cm/16in
Spiraea japonica 'Little Princess'	dwarf with pink flowers	50cm/20in
Taxus cuspidata nana	dwarf upright yew	1m/3ft
Ulmus parviflora pygmea	tiny-leaved elm, good tree shape	30cm/1ft

Forsythia viridissima 'Bronxensis' (above) is a dwarf variety of forsythia that grows to 30cm/12in. It can be grown to look like the large, well-known garden shrub.

Salix lanata 'Stuartii' (right) is a spreading, slow-growing, deciduous shrub that grows to a height of 1m/3ft. Like larger willows, it has catkins in the spring.

in a plant finder directory.

With plenty of thought and inventiveness, there is no reason why you should not miniaturize virtually any sort of garden you fancy — even water gardens and Japanese gardens. But with such specialist styles it can be very difficult — not to mention expensive — to get enough suitably sized plants and accessories with the right proportions to make even the tiniest miniature garden. So three garden styles stand out as being most practi-

cal and each is a successful candidate for miniaturization. They are the traditional formal garden, the alpine garden and the cottage garden.

Formal garden

A formal garden can look wonderful in miniature. Design it just as you would a full-sized garden, but planting compact varieties. You can have dwarf hedges, lawns, miniature trees, shrubs, border plants and annuals – even tiny topiary, all using compact versions of popular, everyday plants.

Box is probably best for low hedges and topiary – it does not mind being kept short and does not need clipping too often. For very short hedges, of around 10-15cm/4-6in, choose the edging box (*Buxus sempervirens* 'Suffruticosa').

Alpine garden

Alpines are particularly appropriate because they are naturally small and allow you to create a tiny but fascinating garden that does not need a lawn to set it off. You do not

even need a rockery as such. A scree garden is more practical to make and usually looks much more 'natural' – you can add a few nicely shaped rocks for decoration.

Grow a mixture of low carpeting plants, bun-shaped hummock plants, dwarf bulbs, tiny mountain trees and shrubs, plus dwarf conifers (small junipers do best in this situation). Ultra dwarf forms of plants such as forsythia,

A scree bed (above) with a selection of small alpine flowers and a dwarf conifer. Many alpines are naturally dwarf in size and are therefore ideal for creating a mini landscape.

elm and willow are 'at home' in a mini alpine garden. They could also be used to create a mini landscape in a trough.

Cottage garden

Since roses are the backbone of a cottage garden, start your planning there, and use whichever type you choose as the basis for the scale of the rest of the planting. The smallest are miniature roses (which grow only 30-45cm/1-1½ft high), followed by patio roses (45-60cm/1½-2ft high) and then some of the smaller English roses. The latter have been deliberately bred to look like old-fashioned roses, but flower all summer – some are only 75-90cm/2½-3ft.

There are few dwarf versions of traditional cottage garden plants. But to get the right effect you can always 'cheat' by replacing them with some of the larger and more 'cottagey' rock-garden plants.

Try dwarf artemisias (for example *A. schmidtiana* 'Nana') for silver foliage, alpine pinks and phlox varieties (more compact than the real cottage garden kind), *Leucanthemum hosmariense* for white ox-eye

GARDEN NOTES

PRUNING AND TRAINING

● Prune mini trees and shrubs lightly in late autumn to improve shape rather than reduce size. You need not aim for a conventional 'lollipop' shape – instead aim for natural craggy shapes which look more interesting.
● Conifers can be lightly clipped to shape; this looks especially good for those with strongly pyramidal or conical shapes. Conifers such as miniature pines, which have open branching shapes, can be pruned rather like large bonsai trees, by removing whole branches or parts of branches to make them look as if their shapes have been formed by the wind.
● Trees, shrubs and conifers can also be trained into shape in spring or summer by holding young branches into the required position with copper wire. Buy the special wire sold for bonsai trees. Anchor the end of the wire firmly round the trunk of the tree and twist the wire round the trunk for a few inches before reaching the branch to be trained. Continue twisting the wire round the branch, with one turn every 1cm/½in, until reaching almost the tip. Then bend the branch gently into position – do not overbend or the branch may snap. Leave the wire in place for a year.

These annual phloxes (left) are all **Phlox drummondii** *in the* **Twinkle Series.** *This group of fairly fast-growing flowers reaches a height of 15cm/6in. They bloom in summer in a wide range of colours. Even shorter species, such as* **P. caespitosa**, *are also available.*

daisy flowers, and rockery campanulas (for example, *C. carpatica*) and geraniums such as *G. sanguineum lancastriense*, *G. cinereum* 'Lawrence Flatman' and *G. dalmaticum*, instead of the much larger herbaceous varieties.

Use violets, sisyrinchiums, soapwort, creeping thymes and tiny sempervivums as authentic small 'fillers'.

Artemisia schmidtiana 'Nana' (left) forms a low mound of silvery-green foliage. It grows to a height of 8cm/3in with a spread of about 20cm/8in.

A tiny formal garden (right) has been created from a camomile lawn with clipped box hedges around miniature roses. This sort of self-contained area can work well as part of a larger garden.

A Green Patch

Wouldn't you love a cool corner to relax and unwind in, away from the tensions of the day? A retreat of green flowers and leaves provides just that.

Green flowers and foliage are one of the most soothing of plant combinations. They are ideal for creating a therapeutic retreat in a quiet corner of the garden – it is almost like growing your own health spa. Green flowers and the sort of striking foliage that goes well with them also provide a wealth of fascinating material for floral artists to use in their arrangements.

Anyone wanting to try their hand at designing with a limited colour scheme will enjoy the challenge of an all-green patch. Hunting for out-of-the-ordinary plants only adds to the thrill. So why not try it in a part of your garden?

A small secluded corner, preferably set slightly apart from the rest of the garden by hedges, walls, fences or a screen of bamboo or shrubs, provides the perfect setting. You can quite easily create such an area by partitioning off a small corner behind trellis panels covered in climbers, perhaps with a small archway leading in.

Designing with greens

From an artistic point of view, colours can be considered to either advance visually or recede. Hot colours, like brilliant orange and yellow, advance, drawing the eye straight to them and creating the impression that the object is closer than it actually is.

Cool colours, like blues and purples, do the opposite. When you look at a distant landscape, the colours furthest from you seem to naturally

disappear into a smoky purple haze. This is what happens when you look at those same colours in the garden; they fool you into thinking the object is further away than it is.

Green lies midway between the two colour groups – it neither advances nor recedes visually. So in an all-green corner, particularly if it is isolated in some way from the rest of the garden, you can create a strong feeling of timelessness and spacelessness which will be extremely relaxing.

This shady brick patio (above) at the end of the garden is coolness itself on a hot, sunny day. Green garden plants filter the sun, while others in containers add exotic interest and variety.

Zinnia 'Envy' (top) has large green flower-heads.

Contrasting leaf shapes and various shades of green have a dramatic effect. Hostas (above) are flanked by variegated grasses.

This sensation is even more pronounced if the green corner is sunken into a natural hollow in the ground. Or try surrounding it with very tall, pale green foliage (such as bamboo), through which the light filters. This will alter the quality of the light, rather as though you were looking out from under water.

An area planted entirely in green could easily become boring, so it needs careful planning. The sort of guidelines used by designers of any horticultural border which concentrates on a single-colour scheme apply here.

Go for contrasts

There are two basic 'ground rules'. Rule One is to make up for the shortage of colour by

ACCOMPANYING FOLIAGE PLANTS

- *Asarum europaeum* – small, leathery, kidney-shaped leaves; evergreen ground cover.
- bamboos: *Arundinaria viridistriata* – gold and green striped leaves; 90cm-1.2m/3-4ft. *A. variegata* – pale green canes with green and white variegated leaves; 1.05m/3½ft. *A. nitida* – thin purplish stems; 3-3.6m/10-12ft. All semi-evergreen, partial shade.
- caper spurge (*Euphorbia lathyris*) – tall, upright plant with strong architectural shape and glaucous foliage; 1.2m/4ft; biennial evergreen flowering in second season; sun or partial shade.
- creeping Jenny (*Lysimachia nummularia* 'Aurea') – mats of ground-hugging, tiny, gold leaves, studded with little yellow flowers in summer; herbaceous; sun to partial shade.
- ferns: shuttlecock or ostrich-feather fern (*Matteuccia struthiopteris* – vase shape with fronds like ostrich feathers radiating out; 60cm/2ft; herbaceous. Northern maidenhair fern (*Adiantum pedatum*) – dainty, cut-leaved fronds; 20cm/8in; herbaceous. Hart's-tongue fern (*Phyllitis scolopendrium* syn. *Asplenium scolopendrium*) – broad, ribbon-like leaves; 45cm/1½ft; evergreen. All moist shade.
- *Geranium renardii* – soft, sage-green, heavily textured leaves forming a mound; 15cm/6in; herbaceous; sun.
- *Gunnera manicata* – giant rhubarb-like leaves, tall prickly stems; 1.8-2.4m/6-8ft; herbaceous; sun.
- *Hakonechloa macra* 'Alboaurea' – graceful, arching, lemon and lime striped grass; 20cm/8in; herbaceous; sun.
- hostas: *Hosta* 'Fringe Benefit' – puckered green leaves bordered white. *H.* 'Gold Standard' – huge gold leaves edged light green. *H.* 'Krossa Regal' – enormous, puckered, fresh green leaves. *H. undulata* 'Mediovariegata' syn. *H.u. undulata* – dwarf with wavy-edged, variegated lime leaves. *H.* 'Golden Medallion' – pale gold, chalice-shaped leaves. All moist soil, sun or shade.
- lamb's tongue (*Stachys olympica* 'Primrose Heron') – lime-green to gold woolly leaves; herbaceous; sun.
- ornamental rhubarb (*Rheum alexandrae*) – huge rhubarb-shaped leaves, yellow bracts; 90cm/3ft; herbaceous; sun.
- sweet woodruff (*Asperula odorata*) – low hillocks of interwoven thread-like leaves; fussy texture makes interesting ground cover; herbaceous; shade.
- *Viburnum rhytidophyllum* – long, leathery, crinkle-textured leaves; 1.8m/6ft; evergreen shrub; sun to partial shade.

using greater contrasts in shape and texture than usual.

Use a mixture of linear shapes like bamboo and iris, coupled with the giant leaves of gunnera or rheum. Or try combining the textured foliage of *Viburnum rhytidophyllum* or *Geranium renardii* with the fluffy flowers of lady's mantle. Perhaps contrast the heart-shaped leaves of hostas with the striking shapes of caper

Lady's mantle (right) has green flowers, as does Helleborus corsicus *(opposite above).* Viburnum rhytidophyllum *(above) has dark evergreen leaves. Interesting when grown singly, they can form a green haven when planted together. The restful corner (far right) combines ferns, hosta, variegated ivy and the red-flowered flame creeper.*

spurge or *Euphorbia wulfenii*.

Use a mixture of plant sizes, too. Large striking plants will create the initial impact, but it is also important to include lots of small details that have to be appreciated in close-up. Curiosities like rose plantain, that you have to bend down to inspect, are unusual and provide variety. Try to keep the garden fresh, always with something new to discover.

Hints of colour

Rule Two is to subtly incorporate the merest hints of a complementary colour to give depth to the scheme. In the famous white garden at Sissinghurst, for instance, you find silver, cream and the merest traces of pale mauve, as well as white.

In a green patch, tiny hints of cream and pale yellow look lovely. You can use a lot of beautiful, variegated foliage,

59

for instance, and it will act as a foil for the green flowers. But when it comes to putting the plants together, don't be in too much of a hurry.

The flower-heads of the spurge family are unusual botanically and in appearance. This one (right) is Euphorbia characias wulfenii, which produces stems of green leaves one year and heads of lime-green flowers the following spring.

Plan the planting

Plant climbers and shrubs first, particularly evergreens as these form the basic all-year-round shape of the planting. Introduce particularly striking foliage plants next. Before planting, test them against different background plants, to find the best effects.

The last step is to add the variegated plants and green flowers to highlight the foliage planting. Aim to put opposites together – small frothy flowers against a background of linear shapes or large glossy leaves, for instance. Try hostas with grasses like the striking, tousled Japanese *Hakonechloa macra* 'Alboaurea'.

Plant large, striking flowers like sea holly (*Eryngium* species) singly or in small groups among fussier foliage. However, use small flowers, like nicotiana, in drifts among giant leaves for maximum impact. Stand the plants together, still in their pots, to judge the effect before finally planting them out.

By planning in advance, it will still be reasonably easy to find the right home for any new plants you come across after the main planting is finished. Just follow the basic guidelines and tuck them into any appropriate gaps.

A green corner can fit neatly into one part of a small town garden (below).

A Balcony Garden

You can create a haven of peace and beauty even in the centre of a bustling city; all you need is the right plants, a little imagination and a balcony.

Balconies come in widely varying shapes, sizes and settings. Some are harsh concrete boxes, others delicate filigree constructions of wrought iron. They can be found clinging to a tower block 30 floors up in the heart of a city or gracing the promenades of seaside towns.

Sadly, balconies are often neglected, becoming a dumping ground for dead houseplants and abandoned skateboards. This need not be so.

Even a few pots planted with the odd pansy and a few pelargoniums will make a difference. And with a little inspiration a balcony can be transformed into a neat place

A large balcony will have room for troughs that can be filled with marigolds, busy Lizzies, pelargoniums and even small trees or shrubs. They will transform the view.

SAFE AND SOUND

SAFETY FIRST

Your balcony must be structurally sound and capable of standing up to a fair amount of weight. Even with light containers and composts, a well-watered pot can be pretty heavy.

It must also have decent drainage. This is not usually a problem as balconies are designed not to collect rainwater. Just make sure that drainage holes and channels are not blocked up.

Last, but certainly not least, ensure that your containers, hanging baskets and trellises are securely fixed. Things fly in all directions in a strong wind. Even the smallest pot can be a serious health-hazard if it falls from a height.

vibrant with life and beauty. The secret lies in what you plant and the way in which you choose to plant it.

Advantages

One of the great pluses of balcony gardening is that you can create the feeling of lush growth far more easily than in a garden. The restricted space enables you to produce a veritable jungle.

Another asset is that it is much easier to keep an eye on things. A balcony protects your treasured plants from free-range pets and the ever-boisterous attentions of children at play.

Certain pests, such as slugs and snails, are deterred by the need to scale such dizzy heights. Even if you bring them in on plants, they can be controlled much more easily than in a garden.

Space is limited on a balcony, so careful thought has to go into how to use it most effectively. For the best results, no surface area should be overlooked.

Tiered containers, such as a handsome strawberry pot, enable you to house lots of plants in the minimum of floor space. They also give you plants growing at an interesting variety of different heights.

Grow climbing plants up walls, and fix hanging baskets,

REDUCING WEIGHT

DON'T FORGET!

Use lightweight containers – plastic and fibreglass rather than stone or terracotta – and aluminium or plastic furniture.

Use peat-based compost. It is much lighter than its soil-based counterpart.

Use small plastic flowerpots or children's play bricks to raise containers off the ground. They are light and allow containers to drain freely.

Shelving (above) is an excellent way of creating space for the maximum number of plants. Trays of vermiculite keep the plants moist and stop the pots dripping. An interesting triangular framework, at left, provides support for several climbers.

A riot of pink and red pelargoniums (left) are seen at their best against an all-white balcony. They are contained in a hanging basket, troughs along the balcony rail and in pots at floor level.

Those lucky enough to have a large balcony on a flat roof (opposite, above right) can be less concerned about the weight of the features they install. Artificial grass enhances the sense of space and highlights the containers.

Clivia miniata (right) blooms in spring and summer. It needs partial shade and a minimum temperature of 10°C/50°F. Bring it indoors before the frosts.

Sunken Gardens

The ideal way to landscape a natural hollow, a sunken garden can also improve a flat site by adding a change of level, privacy and shelter.

...nken gardens have a ...gic of their own. Sitting ...you can relax in your ...vate suntrap, sheltered ...nd, traffic noise and ...ple. The best of them ...ecret gardens.

...gardens were com...res in formal and ...l gardens 50 years ...raditional sunken ...a round or square ...feet lower than ...nding garden. ...own in the stone ...ries shoring up ...d there was a ...l perhaps a for...centre.

...ality

...do not have to ...asic idea be...arden is to ...w in the

A sunken garden can be a central feature or it can be subtly blended in. If your sunken garden has lots of 'hard landscaping' – walls and beds of brick or stone, floors of paving or concrete – it will stand out more (above), at least until the materials have weathered. The sunken garden (right) blends in, although it has steps and flooring of paving stones, because the beds at the sides are a continuation of the surrounding lawn.

decorative wall planters and window boxes to your walls. This not only increases the number of plants but it also takes some weight off the floor and creates space.

Even the ceiling of a balcony can be used. Trailers can hang from it and climbers can be trained over it. You can suspend hanging baskets from the ceiling, as long as you can fix them securely enough to withstand winds.

Design ideas

The right design for your balcony garden depends on what kind of balcony you have and what conditions the plants have to deal with.

An ornate, Georgian style balcony, for example, lends itself to a very formal design. This would suggest stately urns and perhaps a statue or a water feature.

Stone urns are out, because the combined weight of containers, soil, plants and water would be too great. Fibreglass urns solve the problem. They are very light and still look good if tastefully planted. Statues are also available in this material, or you could risk a small stone one.

A water feature need not be a weight problem. Self-contained, wall-mounted water features are becoming popular. They are often in the form of a mask or an animal face that trickles water from its mouth into a shallow basin attached to the wall. This brings the soothing sound of running water to your balcony without its weight.

Seaside design

A seaside balcony lends itself to a much lighter design. A bright and breezy look would fit well with the surroundings. Be sure to incorporate seating into your plan.

Brightly coloured, plastic containers are suitably light and cheerful. You could even continue the seaside theme by using children's buckets, but remember to bore drainage holes in the bottom. A concrete balcony will need to have its harsh lines softened; it will always look best when it is full of plants.

Placing containers

If the balcony is a suntrap, masses of climbers, trailers and bright bedding plants will flourish. Gathering your containers into groups produces

Tiles (above) make it easy to keep the balcony floor clean. Here, troughs have been built into the balcony wall.

Tropaeolum tuberosum 'Ken Aslet' (left) is a lovely climber which is particularly suitable for seaside balconies.

Trellises (right) support climbers that will help shelter your balcony.

A wrought-iron balcony (below) is enhanced by a formal display of flowers.

EXOTIC B...

There are i... alternativ... garden b... followin...
● *Ama...* flowe... and ... flow... 60... fu...

S...
... in one... own pr... from w... other pe... are real s... Sunken... mon featu... semi-forma... ago. The ... garden was ... area severa... the surrou... Plants were g... walls or rock... the sides, an... lawn, a seat an... mal pond in the ...

Inform...
Sunken gardens ... be formal. The ba... hind a sunken g... plant up a holl...

ground. This can suit many different styles of garden.

You could include a small sunken area within an informal or even a wild garden. And a tiny town garden tucked in between tall buildings gives an illusion of being sunken, due to its surroundings.

Siting sunken gardens

All it takes is a little imagination and a few ideas to transform your 'problem' patch into a positive benefit!

It is important to choose a well drained site for a sunken garden, otherwise it can end up being awash all winter.

The best sites are raised up above the level of surrounding land, perhaps within a mound or on a slope. Gravelly or sandy soil is an advantage and the garden should be in a sunny, sheltered area.

Avoid trying to make a sunken garden on heavy clay soil and in places with a high water table, unless you want a bog garden. Check by digging a hole in winter – if it fills with water that doesn't run away, the chances are that you have a high water table.

Traditional style

The traditional, formal sunken garden was situated towards the middle of a larger semi-formal garden, surrounded by grass and paths and by a wall or shrubberies.

To get into the garden, you went down a short flight of steps, and the walls of the sunken area would be of stone or brick. The floor of the garden would have been closely mown grass. In the centre was a round or square pond, with perhaps a fountain or statue, and there were formal beds of annuals or low perennials.

You can recreate this and perhaps make it into a whole garden – it looks good in a small courtyard behind an older town house.

Try adding a formal topiary tree, either in the ground or in a pot, and a seat on some paving slabs. Edging flower beds with dwarf box looks good.

A paved garden

Slightly formal, a paved sunken garden could occupy an entire courtyard behind a town house, or a small front garden. It could also be an isolated feature within a larger garden.

Simply pave the area with bricks, cobbles or slabs, using a pattern that emphasizes the shape of the courtyard. In a round garden, for instance, lay bricks in concentric rings.

CREATING A FORMAL SUNKEN GARDEN

● Choose a circular, oval, square or oblong shape.
● Make it 1.5-1.8m/5-6ft deep, so that your head is below ground level when seated. If the hollow is shallower, add a low wall or hedge around the outside.
● Reinforce the inside of the sunken area with walls of stone or brick.
● For a semi-formal garden, you could make the side walls gently sloping, lined with rockery stone.
● Ensure good drainage in the floor of the garden if you are planting it up. Dig the garden 30cm/12in deeper than you need, then place 5cm/2in of gravel over a 15cm/6in layer of coarse rubble, before replacing a good layer of topsoil.

Add a seat and, round the edge, a low wall or shrubs. Groups of interestingly shaped plants, such as phormium or hardy yucca (*Yucca filamentosa*), will create interest.

A sunken garden in a sunny spot is just the place for rock plants. Either plant them in the dry stone walls that line the sides of a garden, or replace one or all of the walls with a gently sloping rockery.

Rock gardens
Plant sun-loving species in walls that get sun for at least half the day. Reserve small hardy ferns and crevice-dwelling shade-lovers, like ramonda and haberlea, for the north-facing side.

You can pave the floor of the garden, or make a series of gravel paths between raised beds or small, natural-looking rocky outcrops. You could also add a seat on a small area of paving, with a collection of sink gardens nearby.

Mediterranean style
Mediterranean herbs, silver leaved perennials and slightly tender plants, such as perennial salvias, gazanias, osteospermum, pelargoniums and many other brightly coloured species, all do well in a sunny sunken garden. The more tender species, such as gazanias and pelargoniums, will, however, need to be overwintered in a frost-free place.

The style can be formal or informal, depending on how you lay it out.

Whichever you choose, remember that these kinds of plants need good drainage. Plant them in the walls or sloping rockery, in raised beds or in urns or other containers, rather than in the ground.

Use paving or gravel for the garden floor – the reflected heat and light are beneficial.

Wild gardens
A sunken wild garden should be very natural in style. It could be crammed full of flowers, with just the odd path wending its way through. And there might be a tiny clearing of shredded bark with a fallen log to sit on.

Or you could have a wildflower lawn. Choose species that thrive in moist conditions

A BOG GARDEN

A bog garden is the ideal way to plant up a sunken garden on wet soil. Go for a natural style and use moisture-loving plants such as *Inula, Buphthalmum,* candelabra primula, *Iris laevigata* hybrids, the corkscrew rush (*Juncus effusus* 'Spiralis'), mimulus, marsh marigold and purple loosestrife.

BRIGHT IDEAS

GOING FOR AN INFORMAL STYLE

- Leave natural hollows unaltered as far as possible.
- Choose a simple, flowing shape when creating an artificial hollow.
- Avoid fussy shapes with lots of convolutions, or the edges of the garden are likely to be weak.
- Make the sides slope gently; this looks more natural and they are much easier to plant.
- Reinforce sides with rockery stones or dry stone walling. You can also terrace them, making a series of level beds, each with a low retaining wall.
- Reinforce the rim of the garden with paving over proper foundations, well concreted in place. Alternatively, plant heavily round the rim to deter people from walking too close to the edge.
- Aim for a slightly uneven floor, rather than one which is entirely flat, and therefore unnatural looking.

Gazanias (opposite top) will bring a vivid splash of colour to a corner of your sunken garden. Except in very mild areas, they are best treated as annuals. This variety is Gazania 'Freddie'.

Salvias (left) are members of the sage family. The many varieties include annuals, biennials, perennials and even evergreen shrubs. They have showy flowers and are ideal for a bed in a sunken garden. This one is Salvia sylvestris 'Mainacht'.

Whether your sunken garden is formal, as here (above), or informal, it should have a comfortable bench or seat in a sunny corner out of the wind.

If your entire garden is on a slope, or you have a slope within the garden, you can create a sunken garden within a natural fold of the land (right).

if the base of your sunken garden is wet in winter. Around this you might have slightly raised flower beds edged with logs, containing taller species arranged naturally in clumps.

If you have a large, dell-like hollow, gently sloping grass banks could lead into the garden, with a choice of paths winding their way down. Plant the bends with drifts of tall flowers, such as rosebay willowherb, or with native bushes like *Viburnum opulus*, so that the view below reveals itself gradually.

A sunken garden should be a private haven and a restful place which is always a delight to visit.

Budget Gardens

Watching the pennies? Sensible money-saving tips can help you hang onto your cash without sacrificing results in any area of the garden.

With a little planning and effort, your borders can be an exciting mix of interesting plants and colours. All these plants (above) could have been bought ready-grown from a garden centre. At much less expense, however, you can grow them yourself from seed or tubers or propagate them from cuttings taken from the gardens of friends and relatives. There is real satisfaction in looking at a lovely border of plants that you have nurtured from scratch.

Gardening doesn't have to be an expensive hobby. With judicious recycling, some good gardening friends, a bit of patience and basic DIY skills, you can have a garden quite as good as your neighbours' for a fraction of the price.

Growing your own plants from seed or cuttings saves money and is fun. But don't economize on proper sowing and cuttings compost – this is one thing you cannot do without. Garden soil, even if sterilized, is not a good enough propagating medium.

Take cuttings

Get cuttings from friends; not just of pot plants, geraniums and fuchsias, but of shrubs, roses and hedging plants as well. A book on propagation will tell you what sort of cuttings to take from which plants and when to take them for best results. Take cuttings of your own plants too.

Strike cuttings of half hardy perennials in pots in late summer and keep them on a window-sill indoors for the winter. This works for verbena, pelargonium, fuchsia, penstemon and many others and is much cheaper than buying new plants every spring. When you buy a new plant – for indoors or out – take cuttings and give some to a friend. That way, if your plant dies you always know where to go for a free replacement!

STORING SEED

To keep opened packets of seeds from one year to the next, fold the top down and store in an airtight container with a sachet of silica gel (from chemists and photographic shops) to absorb moisture. Keep in a cool, dark place, at a steady temperature.

The longer you store seed, the lower the germination rate will be, so sow stored seed more thickly than usual to compensate. Don't bother storing parsnip, salsify or scorzonera seed – they only come up well the year they are bought.

BRIGHT IDEAS

70

Rooted pelargonium cuttings (above) will form a lovely summer display. Take 8cm/ 3in tip cuttings from standards in midsummer and from large bush types in early autumn. Overwinter in a light, frost-free place.

Propagate stinking iris (Iris foetidissima) from its seeds (right) or by dividing its rhizomes.

Collect ripe seeds from your hellebores (below right) during the summer.

RECYCLING TIPS

- Compost all kitchen and garden waste to make your own free soil improver.
- When enlarging flower beds, strip off and stack the turves for loam to make your own potting composts.
- Sterilize leaf mould and other ingredients for potting composts in roasting bags in an oven set at the lowest temperature (50°C/122°F) for 1½ hours. Sterilize all ingredients separately before mixing the compost, then spread them out in trays to 'breathe' for a few days before use.
- Buy second-hand garden tools from junk shops, jumble sales or car boot sales. You can get broken tools cheaply re-handled at some tool shops, or you can buy the handles and do it yourself.
- Swap gardening magazines with a friend.
- Make tree ties from lengths of hosepipe with wire threaded through.
- Re-use plastic vending machine cups as pots (make a hole in the base with a hot skewer).
- Re-use fruit punnets as seed trays; transparent plastic supermarket meat/veg trays make good propagator lids.
- Save old tights to hang up shallots and onions to store for winter.
- Save fruit tree prunings to use as pea sticks next year.
- Instead of buying new plant labels each year, clean the old ones with wire wool and washing up liquid and re-use them.

Work out seed orders with friends. Then you can share a packet of cabbage seeds, for instance, instead of buying a packet each. Or get several friends to each grow a few packets of seed, and share the plants with the whole group. And if buying a lot of seed, look out for special collections (particularly of vegetable seeds) which are sometimes offered in seed catalogues.

Saving seed

When sowing, do not use the entire packet of seed at once – you'll end up with far more plants than you need. Instead, sow a small pinch and use the rest for successional sowings, or save it for next year.

If you feel adventurous, try saving seed from your own plants. Seeds worth saving are those of trees and shrubs, peas, beans, bulbs and flowers other than F1 hybrid varieties. Allow the pods to dry right out on the plant; gather fruits and berries when they are overripe and fall naturally from the plant. Remove seed from pods, and wash the flesh from seeds of fruit or berries.

Sow or swap tree and shrub seed immediately after collection for best results. Store that of annuals and vegetables in an airtight container, ready for sowing the next spring.

Join a society

A good local gardening club is well worth the membership fee. Clubs often negotiate a discount for their members at local garden centres. And by ordering as a group, you can get substantial discounts on seeds and bulbs from some of the large companies.

Some clubs even have their own trading hut to sell fertilizers and other gardening items at special rates. Many own and lend out the sort of equipment you only use once in a while, like fertilizer spreaders or powered lawn rakers. Club 'bring and buy' sales are a cheap source of plants, and a good way of disposing of your surplus stock.

Some national societies can also be good value. The Royal Horticultural Society, Alpine Garden Society and Hardy Plant Society all run seed dis-

PROJECT MAKE YOUR OWN 'STONE'

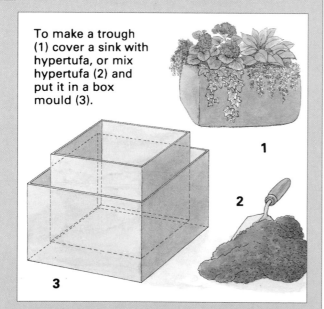

To make a trough (1) cover a sink with hypertufa, or mix hypertufa (2) and put it in a box mould (3).

1

2

3

Make your own garden containers, ornaments and even fake rock from hypertufa. Simply mix together equal parts of peat, sharp sand and cement with enough water to make it sticky.

To make fake rocks, urns, sculptures or other ornaments cover a shape made from scrunched up wire netting with hypertufa. Or use it to give a fake stone finish to an old glazed sink (spread an outdoor adhesive over the glaze first to give it something to grip to).

You can make your own containers by using two cardboard boxes, one slightly smaller than the other. Place a 4cm/1½in layer of mixture in the base of the bigger box and stand the second inside it, leaving a gap all round the edges. Fill this with more of the mixture. When the mixture is thoroughly set (after several weeks) tear the cardboard away.

Spring is the time to sow hardy annual seeds in the garden (above). Collect the ripe seed from your plants in autumn and store it in an airtight container over the winter.

There is no need to buy a lot of different fertilizers for your garden plants. Manufacturers, of course, are in the business of selling as many different products as they can. All you actually need are two liquid or soluble fertilizers – one general purpose and one high in potash – and a good dry fertilizer, such as Growmore (above right).

The decision to buy power tools will depend on your budget and how much time and energy you have to spend in the garden. An electric lawn-raker (left) will make short work of removing moss and dead grass from your lawn and is probably worth the investment and running costs if you have a large area of grass. The alternatives are to spend longer using an inexpensive lawn rake or to borrow or hire a machine when you need one.

GROWMORE

BONE MEAL

FISH, BLOOD AND BONE

tribution schemes which allow members to draw a number of packets of free seed as a 'perk' of membership.

Buying garden products

Choose a few general purpose products you can use all round the garden, instead of lots of specialized ones. A versatile fertilizer like Growmore or Blood, Fish and Bone can be used on lawns, flowers and vegetables, both as a pre-planting feed and during the growing season.

Two liquid or soluble feeds – one general purpose and the other high in potash (tomato feed) – are all you need for house and greenhouse plants, tubs and hanging baskets.

Do not buy pesticides and fungicides unless you need them. For small infestations, just wipe mildew or greenfly away with a damp cloth. If you do need chemicals, trigger packs can be the best value in small gardens as you do not need to buy a sprayer, and

nothing goes to waste – you just spray what you need. In a larger garden, it is cheaper to buy a concentrate and dilute it ready for use.

You should be able to manage without weedkillers entirely. Hand weeding and hoeing are cheaper and environmentally safer. And by making your own compost, you can be sure of a regular free supply of material for soil improvement and mulching.

If you also collect dead leaves to make leafmould and stack turves for loam, you can even make your own potting mixtures. A good all-purpose recipe is equal parts of sterilized loam, sharp sand and leafmould or cocopeat. Add a slow-release fertilizer, following the maker's instructions, and mix everything well and use it when fresh.

Buying tools

Avoid gadgets; stick to a few good quality basic tools – a spade, fork, hand trowel and

hoe. Electric mowers are a good buy for small lawns. They are cheaper initially and do not need expensive servicing like petrol mowers.

When you have all the tools and equipment you need, look after them properly to get the maximum working life. Clean and dry tools after use, and paint the blades or prongs with oil to prevent rusting (old sump oil from the car is ideal).

Clean dead grass out from under the mower after use, and oil hedge trimmers and shears. Finally, keep the garden shed locked – thefts of garden equipment are common, and may not be covered by your household insurance.

HANDY HINTS

- Watch out for end of season sales at nurseries and garden centres.
- Grow your own garden canes by planting tall species of bamboo (if you have space), or the ornamental sugar cane *Miscanthus* which has bamboo-like stems. Cut stems after two years when they are hard.

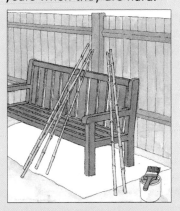

- Treat bamboo canes, wooden posts and fence panels, timber greenhouse frames and hardwood garden furniture with timber preservative every year to prolong their life.
- Bring cushions from garden seats indoors when not in use to prevent fading in sunlight, and store in a dry place in winter to prevent them mildewing.
- Paint handles of small tools like trowels and secateurs orange so they don't get lost if you put them down in the garden.

An Alpine Sink Garden

A miniature alpine garden is easy to make and will last for years. Neatly contained, it makes a charming focal point.

All you need for a really individual container garden is a stone trough or an old sink. An alpine sink garden looks good in almost any setting, takes very little time to make and requires the minimum of care and maintenance – just regular watering during the growing season.

First, find your container. Alpine troughs made from reconstituted stone are available from most garden centres, but at a price. Better still (and cheaper), use an old-fashioned porcelain sink. If you are willing to scavenge from derelict houses, factories or even an old hospital, you may be lucky enough to discover a discarded porcelain sink ready for the taking. Such finds, though, are rare. You may be better advised to ask a local builder who renovates old houses to look out for one for you. Junk yards and architectural salvage companies are further possible sources, but they may charge you more.

An 'antique' sink

Giving an old porcelain sink an 'antique stone' finish is a simple process. After scoring the smooth surface by chipping it with a hammer or using an electric drill fitted with a coarse carborundum disk, paint it with a bonding agent. When this is tacky, slap on a mixture of equal parts of sand, cement and peat, building it up to a layer approximately 1cm/½in thick. Leave the sink for a few days to dry completely, before planting.

The sink will soon take on a weathered appearance, but this can be accelerated by painting it with liquid manure, boiled rice water or natural yoghurt, which encourages the growth of algae and moss.

Site your sink

Once you have found your sink, decide where you want to site it: on the patio, perhaps, under a window or in the corner of your lawn? You should also decide whether you want to leave it as it is or – particularly if it is cracked or chipped

A LANDSCAPE IN MINIATU[RE]

A patio or paved area provides the ideal location for a sink garden

Encourage lichen to grow on the trough, for an 'antique' effect

When selecting the planting positions make sure plants will have enough room to spread

Some plants, like this Sempervivum grandiflorum, will grow happily in the compost-filled crevices of rocks

A layer of grit or shingle around the base of the plants looks attractive and is essential to prevent rotting and to conserve moisture

A sink garden provides you with the ideal opportunity to exercise your creativity. Here (above) a wonderful selection of dainty alpines, dwarf conifers and succulent, fleshy plants have been carefully selected to flourish on and around a few well-chosen rocks. The resulting effect is one of a harmonious landscape in miniature.

– whether you wish to 'antique' the outside to resemble an old stone trough. Move the sink to its permanent position now as it will be too heavy to move once it is filled with compost.

Good drainage, the correct soil or compost mixture and carefully chosen plants are the most vital considerations. If you begin with the best ingredients you will keep your sink garden looking happy and

Dwarf conifers, such as Sawara cypress, will give height to your planting scheme

A few well-placed rocks create an interesting mini-landscape effect

Select plants with a variety of leaf shapes and colours

Raise the sink above ground level to improve drainage from the sink or trough

hoose plants with fferent flowering mes for all year und interest and olour

Instead of selecting lots of different plants to fill your trough garden, select just one variety for a stunning and full effect. The dazzling white saxifrage (right) 'Tumbling Waters' cascades gracefully over the edge of the trough softening the edges as it grows. This plant thrives in a well-drained trough but the roots must not be allowed to dry out. Water daily, if necessary, in dry conditions.

the hole with a piece of folded small-meshed netting.)

Put a layer of coarse gravel or broken clay pots (crocks) in the bottom, to a depth of at least 2.5cm/1in. Cover this with a 5cm/2in layer of well-rotted garden compost or composted tree bark.

Compact compost

Fill the sink to within 6mm/½in of the rim with good quality soil or John Innes No 2 potting compost. Create a slight mound in the centre to prevent the soil from 'dipping' when it is first watered and

to improve drainage.

For the best results, buy compost from a garden centre or nursery. Most garden soil does not contain enough nutrients to keep container-grown plants happy and healthy. Garden soil has a different texture too and is also more likely to set in a solid lump after it has received a good soaking.

As you put the compost into the sink, press it down fairly firmly. This will allow the plants' roots to become firmly anchored and also ensures the compost level will not settle

healthy for many years.

Drainage is very important: container plants need frequent watering but if water cannot drain away, your plants will soon become waterlogged. To prevent this, first stand your sink or trough on a stable base of bricks or blocks.

If you are using a sink, cut away the wastepipe but leave the strainer over the plug hole. (If the plug is missing, cover

Troughs come in all shapes and sizes and this oval one (right) has been sunk into a border. Here, several different varieties of the same plant have been chosen in complementary colours.

Sempervivums come in deep, dark red and fresh, bright green. Some types display contrasting colours on the tips of their succulent leaves.

A profusion of piercing blue contrasts splendidly with the stark grey rocks and gravel (left). Spring gentian (Gentiana verna) loves the environment created by a sink garden, as long as it is well drained. The dainty flowers emerge in early spring, their five petals are joined to a white, tubular neck and are borne on short upright stems.

too much after watering.

Before planting up, lay your chosen plants on the surface and rearrange them until you are happy with the total look of your miniature garden. Attention to height and colour is particularly important with such a small area to design. Do not be tempted to cram in too many plants or they will not have space to settle and spread.

Large rocky stones, specially for alpine gardens, can be bought from garden centres. They are pieces of 'tufa', a porous limestone on which many alpine plants can thrive. Try to create a natural effect with the stones sloping gently and most of the undersides buried in the compost.

Once you have planted up the sink, cover the exposed soil between the alpines with a 6mm/½in layer of gravel, small pebbles or fine shingle. This is not only attractive but helps to stop the container from drying out too quickly. It also keeps the plants' leaves away from the damp soil which prevents them rotting. Water in well after planting.

After a while – it could be months or years – you may decide you have not achieved the desired effect. Do not despair; it is easy to replace individual

WHICH PLANTS?

Here are a dozen rockery perennials which are ideal for sink gardens. Make your own selection, contrasting shape, colour and foliage.

- common houseleek *(Sempervivum tectorum)* — rosette-shaped succulent with rosy-purple flowers. Evergreen perennial
- stonecrop *(Sedum spathulifolium)* — low-growing evergreen with grey-green leaf rosettes that form dense mats; yellow flowers
- stonecrop *(S. spurium)* — creeping evergreen with mid-green leaves and red stems; pink, white or red flowers
- aubrieta *(Aubrieta deltoidea)* — spreading, mat-forming plant with crimson, purple or pink flowers; can be invasive
- glory of the snow *(Chionodoxa lucilae)* — spring-flowering bulb with narrow leaves and sprays of blue and white flowers
- saxifrage *(Saxifraga species)* — low-growing plant forming compact hummocks; red, pink, white, yellow or purple flowers
- rock phlox *(Phlox douglasii)* — carpeting semi-evergreen with white, pink or lavender starry flowers and oval leaves
- spring gentian *(Gentiana verna* 'Angulosa') — lime-loving plant forming tufts of spiky leaves with bright blue flowers
- rock pink *(Dianthus* 'La Bourbille') — dwarf cousins of the border pink, hardy, with showy pink flowers
- Sawara cypress *(Chamaecyparis pisifera* 'Nana Aureovariegata') — dwarf conical evergreen with a golden sheen
- Lawson's cypress *(C. lawsoniana* 'Minima Aurea') — dwarf rounded evergreen
- common juniper *(Juniperus communis* 'Compressa') — dwarf juniper with needle-like aromatic leaves

1 *Place a 2.5cm/1in layer of crocks in the bottom of the trough to help drainage. Add John Innes No. 2 compost.*

2 *Fill to within 6mm/½in of the rim. Press compost down firmly to prevent it settling when watered and to give plants a good anchorage.*

5 *Arrange the plant pots before planting to make the most of colour, height and texture.*

6 *Remove each plant from its container, tease out the root ball gently and set in position.*

plants or even to start again from scratch. Slow-growing plants, for instance, may eventually become too large for your sink. Choose carefully, as many plants will last for as much as five years or longer.

Bit of a boost

When replacing individual plants, remove as much soil as possible without disturbing the other plants and replace it with fresh soil or compost, to give the whole container a boost. This technique is known as top dressing. If you are replanting completely after some years, replace all the compost to give new plants the best possible chance.

All container-grown plants need generous feeding as the nutrients in the compost can become exhausted after only a few months. As a general rule, feed fortnightly with a balanced liquid fertilizer during the growing season. Always apply fertilizer after watering and never feed plants in hot sun as they may scorch.

During a hot summer you may need to water your sink garden once or even twice a day. The compost should never be allowed to dry out completely and always give enough water to soak right through to the container's base.

LPINE SINK GARDEN

3 Arrange attractive stones or special alpine rocks, positioning them carefully to create maximum impact.

4 Plants which require good drainage should be set at the edges of the sink, where water drains well.

7 Cover all the exposed soil with gravel, small pebbles or fine shingle to a depth of 6mm/½ in.

8 Give the sink a thorough soaking using a watering can with a fine rose. Regular watering is vital.

This stonecrop, Sedum spathulifolium (above), is a carpeter which has rosettes of succulent silvery-green leaves. Small clusters of yellow star-shaped flowers appear intermittently creating an interesting mottled effect.

Saxifraga moschata (below) forms a neat hummock of olive green, spiky rosettes. Graceful flowers in all shades of pink sit on elegant red stems.

In the Shade

If you have a corner that doesn't see the light, there is a wide range of shade-loving plants to bring it beautifully to life.

Think of the shade in your garden as an advantage! Many plants thrive in cool places and are under less stress from water loss. Early spring-flowering bulbs are at their best in shade, and camellias prefer shade because early morning winter sun can damage their leaves and petals.

Woodland plants grow best under the cover of trees. For a pretty show of spring flowers, primroses, bergenia, hellebore, Solomon's seal, bleeding heart, pulmonaria and periwinkle all do well in shade.

Well contained

You can grow fairly large shrubs and even small trees in containers in the shade. Bulbs and spring and summer bedding plants also perform well in such conditions. There are, however, several key factors for successful plants in a contained environment. You will have to provide them with the right growing medium, adequate water, fertilizer and, if necessary, winter protection. Choose your plants according to the size of container and your own seasonal favourites.

Being choosy

Although you can grow many of these plants from seed, it will take some time before they are large enough to make an impression in a container. It is therefore better to buy young plants from garden centres or nurseries.

Choose your container for the look you want to create, considering the number of plants and their ultimate size. In a garden setting or patio,

stone urns, terracotta pots, sinks, old baths and iron water tanks can all be used for a variety of effects. On a balcony, where stone containers may be too heavy when filled, you may like to consider lightweight plastic replica versions.

This imposing terracotta tub gives a sunny display even though it is in the shade. There are a wide range of leaf colours and shapes to add interest and the yellow tobacco plant is night scented too.

When you begin to prepare the container for planting, place it in position before you fill it with soil and plants. You can then see what it looks like before it becomes too heavy.

Make sure that your container has drainage holes in

the base. Before you add soil, make a good drainage layer. Place a layer of crocks in the bottom of the container, then cover this layer with clean gravel. Water the containers regularly – preferably every day – when they are planted up, particularly during prolonged hot, dry weather.

Good drainage

Containers planted under trees should be lined with plastic before planting so that a reservoir of water is held in the base. Plant up as normal, with a layer of drainage material. The water will then drain away from the roots and prevent them rotting, but is stored so that it is available when the plants need it.

To promote good growth, use a soil-based compost and mix in fertilizer before you plant the container. In spring, loosen the surface of the container,

Herald the spring in even the dullest of corners by planting up lots of pots with bulbs. Instead of mixing plants stick to one type and colour in each one. Simple terracotta pots (right) are transformed by dazzling white hyacinths and vibrant yellow daffodils.

Creating a look that is completely different, this white chair (below) makes an unusual pedestal for a plant display – and helps drainage. Trailing ivy softens the edges of an elegant grecian style trough. The overgrown trellis creates a shaded environment which is used here to best advantage.

if it is a large one, and add a top-dressing of new compost. For plants that prefer acid soils use a proprietary lime-free or ericaceous compost which contains the correct balance of nutrients.

Colour planning

For the brightest burst of early colour some of the most rewarding container-grown plants are spring-flowering bulbs. Prepare your containers in the autumn; you could, for instance, plant up small terracotta pots with tulips. Plant two or three winter-flowering pansies in each pot. The pansies will supply colour through the winter and in spring the bulbs will flower through the pansy mounds.

Although one large shrub can look very effective in a pot, why not surround it with flowers to give a new effect with each season? Plant small bulbs, like allium or snake's head fritillary (*Fritillaria meleagris*) around the edge and leave them undisturbed. When they have finished flowering

they will only look untidy for a few weeks until their foliage dies back. In the centre of the container plant a permanent shrub such as camellia. In spring sow trailing lobelia seeds around the shrub. In summer they will tumble over

the edge of the pot and make a colourful groundcover. Camellias like a lime-free or acid soil, so top-dress them after flowering with an ericaceous compost.

The dramatic strap-like

SHADY SHRUBS	FLOWERS AND FOLIAGE
Japanese azaleas	Evergreen; many flower colours. Acid lover
Camellia japonica and × *williamsia* varieties	Evergreen; many flower colours. Acid lover
Skimmia japonica	Evergreen; needs male and female plants
Mahonia aquifolium	Evergreen; yellow flowers, purple berries
floribunda roses	Many flowers
Pieris formosa	Evergreen; red leaves in spring; white flowers. Acid lover

CLIMBERS AND WALL SHRUBS	FLOWERS AND FOLIAGE
flowering quince	Spring flowers
Hydrangea petiolaris	White lace-cap flowers
'*Zephirine Drouhin' rose	Perfumed. Dead head for long flowering
*winter-flowering jasmine	Delicate yellow flowers on bare stems
*summer-flowering jasmine	White perfumed flowers, feathery leaves
Clematis alpina	Spring flowers
Clematis 'Nelly Moser'	Large pink flowers
Clematis macropetala	Bell-shaped blue flowers
ivies	Evergreen; wide range of leaf colours and shapes.
holly	Evergreen; variegated or plain leaves. Berries
firethorn	Evergreen; clusters of small flowers. Bright berries
cotoneaster	Evergreen; tiny flowers, berries

* These climbers need the support of trellis, stakes or wires

If you have only enough room for one container plant then this evergreen Pieris formosa 'Forrestii' (above) is an excellent choice. Its young leaves are brilliant red and it produces clusters of white flowers in the spring so there is always something new to look out for.

These colourful flowers (below) seem to cascade down the steps. With a pot positioned on each step the plants mingle and hide the containers.

leaves of New Zealand flax (*phormium tenax*), offers a striking fan-shaped outline and good colour all year round. There are many different coloured forms including some with purple to bronze foliage, others are striped yellow and green. Protect it in hard winters by spreading a straw mulch around its feet and wrap it with hessian sacking.

Climbing plants

Many climbing plants do well in containers in shady corners. They will not be as rampant as they might in a sunnier position, but they offer colourful cover for walls. Climbers can also be coaxed up trees.

The climbing hydrangea,

Hydrangea petiolaris, likes shade but is a slow starter. Once it gets going, however, it provides a show of pretty lace-cap flowers and glossy green leaves.

Shady scents

Some climbing roses, too, do just as well in shade as in sun. Perfume, lovely flowers and pretty foliage in spring are their gifts to the garden. Flowering from spring until autumn, the thornless rose, 'Zephirine Drouhin', is unbeatable. Make sure that it is well supported by canes in the container and remove all faded flower heads promptly to keep a succession of flowers going.

For a complete summer and

winter picture plant a large container with the dainty, yellow-flowered winter jasmine, *Jasminum nudiflorum*, and the white-flowered summer jasmine, *Jasminum officinale*. They both perform well in shade, have delicate foliage and pretty fragrance.

Clematis is a favourite garden plant and many do grow well in containers in the shade. They all like a cool root run and plenty of moisture. *C. macropetala* flowers later in spring making a pretty cover as it tumbles over the edges of the container. Of the large-flowered clematis varieties 'Nelly Moser' is best as it keeps its colour better in shade.

Evergreen favourites

Evergreens are a great advantage in shady situations. They do not always have green foliage: some have mixed white and green colourings or variegations and some have attractive buttery golden markings.

Bear in mind, however, that in dense shade they may not be as bright as they would be in a sunnier situation. Many evergreens have brightly coloured berries in autumn, lasting through the winter.

Holly, firethorn and cotoneaster suit container growth in shady corners. Ivy can be used to brighten and soften shady

PROJECT PLANTING UP POTS

Select the position for the container before adding soil. Make sure the tub has drainage holes in the base. Place a layer of crocks in the bottom and cover with a layer of gravel. Use a soil-based compost and mix in a little fertilizer before you plant. Arrange the plants then firm into position. Water well.

spots and comes in a wide range of leaf colours and shapes. Depending on which ivy you choose you can use it to tumble over containers or climb up walls, trellis and trees. *Hedera colchica* 'Sulphur Heart' (sometimes sold as 'Paddy's Pride') has a yellow splash of colour in the centre of its leaves. Give it a cane or trellis support when you plant it in a container under a tree

Delicate flowers may survive in shady corners as shade and shelter often go hand in hand. An exquisite selection of plants (below) in fragile, subtle colours makes a permanent floral arrangement. Silvery trailing Helichrysum petiolatum, petunias, lobelia and daisy-like chrysanthemums look wonderful together.

BRIGHT IDEAS

SHADY SPOTS

- A shady stairway down to a basement flat is an ideal situation for a series of pots. Create a mass of colour or select just one.
- If you have an old tree in a shady spot, cloak it in clematis.
- On a shady windowsill, plant up a window box with bright violas and ivies, for long-lasting colour and interest. In the winter, use winter-flowering varieties of viola.

and it will soon climb strongly. For a reddish-purple colour in winter use *Hedera helix* 'Atropurpurea'. Its dark leaves turn a bronze to purple colour in winter.

Foliage and flowers

Many shrubs have such lovely foliage that their flowers almost pale into insignificance. The spotted laurel, *Aucuba*

japonica, has glossy green leaves and bright red berries in autumn. *A.j.* 'Maculata' has bright, yellow-splashed leaves. The flowers, small, green and star-shaped, appear in spring. For a bolder colour effect, underplant the container with daffodil bulbs in autumn. In spring they will make a stunning display against the glossy leaves and star shaped flowers of the aucuba.

Floribunda roses look good in containers on a patio or balcony. They need to have a good deal of space for their roots, so make sure the container you use is at least 38cm/15in deep. Dwarf floribundas, too, can be used for a colourful display in a container. Provide good drainage and never let the container get water-logged. Feed roses twice a year, when spring growth is beginning and again in mid-summer. In return they will provide a bright spot for a shady corner.

Wigwams

For a crop of tasty runner beans or a swathe of colourful sweet peas, try this original and space-saving idea.

To get the most from a small garden you need to use space to maximum advantage. Think of limited space not as a barrier to creative gardening, but as a challenge.

You may not have room for a vegetable garden, but that need not deter you from growing a healthy crop of runner beans or tall-growing peas. A wigwam-shaped structure can be fitted into any small space – the corner of a flower bed, a balcony, patio or even a flat roof garden – and will enable you to grow a number of vegetables or flowering plants.

Getting started

A wigwam is cheap and easy to construct to almost any size. You can use a variety of materials, depending on the size and weight of the plants you want to grow. Bamboo poles, pea sticks and even strong twigs are all suitable.

Wigwams in containers are a good way to expand your garden onto the patio or balcony, creating an unusual feature and adding a touch of colour. Take care in choosing a container that is large enough to support the fully grown plants without toppling over.

Perfect proportions

Your wigwam must be strong enough to support the plants. Make sure it is not so large, though, that the contents will look out of proportion with the container in which it stands.

Very vigorous perennials, like some forms of clematis and rambling roses, make striking features but need strong supports. They are unsuitable for all but the largest of containers.

Good containers for tall plants include half barrels, deep sinks and troughs. You can also use large plastic pots weighted at the bottom with heavy rocks or broken bricks. Mini-wigwams, which support smaller annual flowers, are ideal for less bulky containers.

In the garden

You can put your wigwam in any area of the garden large enough to house a circle of a minimum of 75cm/2ft 6in in diameter. Use your wigwam constructively and situate it where it will hide an eyesore like a garden shed or compost bin. Bear in mind that once the plants are growing strongly your wigwam will take on a

GROWING TIPS

BE CREATIVE

● Mix and match – runner beans and sweet peas can look good together or try different annuals on the same wigwam.
● Runner beans don't always have red flowers. Look out for pink 'Sunset', white 'Desiree' or even red and white 'Painted Lady'. Grow them separately or together.
● The runner bean 'Purple Podded' is pretty and delicious.
● Experiment with different shaped wigwams — ovals, triangles or rectangles. Don't bend each cane too much however as it may snap. If you can't gather the canes at the top try tying them to a short horizontal cane.

Wigwams are a great space saver in the vegetable garden. These tall bamboo structures (above) are not only bound at the top, they also have strings wound round them in a spiral from top to bottom, to provide added support for peas and beans.

solid appearance. So when you select the position try to place it behind smaller plants.

When your wigwam is thickly covered in foliage, rain will have difficulty getting to the centre so give the plants regular long drinks.

First decide what you want to grow up your wigwam. For

and help to prevent your beans drying out in hot weather. Then dig in some well-rotted manure or garden compost to enrich the ground.

Water your bean plants twice a week throughout the flowering and pod-growing season, directing the water at the base of the plants and not at the flowers and foliage. Adequate watering is essential to produce a good crop, but do not keep the soil saturated as it could cause root rot.

Round in circles

The size of your wigwam will depend on what you grow up it. For beans and larger perennials use 2-2.5m/7-8ft heavy grade bamboo canes which will support the weight of these fairly heavy plants. Place one upright in the centre and arrange the others in a circle around it, 15-30cm/6-12in apart. Push the ends firmly into the ground and tie

These sweet peas (above) will grow right to the top of this 1.5m/5ft wigwam, making a pretty and compact display, as well as providing a good stock of flowers for cutting.

annual or perennial flowers simply dig the ground over and add a little general fertilizer. If you choose climbing French or runner beans, prepare the ground by digging it over and placing layers of wet newspapers about 45cm/18in below the surface. These will hold moisture when you water

Here is positive proof that a wigwam can be used for a decorative as well as a practical purpose. A container-grown clematis (left) can be trained into a neat, conical shape with just a bit of prudent pruning.

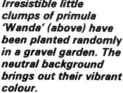

Irresistible little clumps of primula 'Wanda' (above) have been planted randomly in a gravel garden. The neutral background brings out their vibrant colour.

It is a lovely surprise to come across the small evergreen perennial Armeria juniperifolia which is almost camouflaged by the large pieces of gravel. A host of colours and textures are captured in the irregular stones.

combines well with many kinds of paving, for instance. Instead of paving a whole area, leave a portion unpaved and fill it with gravel – it will probably reduce the cost and improve the appearance. Or make a striking design by leaving regular areas unpaved and filling them with two or three different types or colours of gravel.

Do not be tempted to overdo it though, as too many types or colours of gravel or paving will look fussy.

A sunken garden

A sunken garden can bring character and interest to a garden, rather like creating a small garden 'room' to explore, and using gravel gives the advantage of better drainage. Whereas in a paved area surface water can be a problem after heavy rain, gravel allows free drainage. Also, because there are natural boundaries to retain the gravel, it never

MAINTENANCE

The beauty of gravel is that it requires so little upkeep. If you lay it on polythene, the weeds that grow near the surface will die off quickly. Light hoeing will take care of most weeds, or use a weedkiller specially formulated for paths. One application should last all season. There are several available and most will not 'creep' through the soil to harm established plants, but do take care not to apply it too close to plants. Be prepared to use a 'spot' weedkiller on weeds that persistently reappear.

strays into surrounding beds.

Be prepared, though, because the creation of a sunken garden will no doubt involve a lot of heavy excavation.

Brilliant backdrops

If your interest lies more in plants than in creating eye-catching features, there are several ways in which gravel

SIX OF THE BEST

You can grow most of the more vigorous alpines in areas of gravel, but it is best to start with some of the large, bold and bright plants that will not give up and die if you happen to tread on them occasionally, and that will give a good display over a long period, from spring until autumn.

● Thrift (*Armeria maritima*) forms evergreen grass-like tufts, covered in spring and early summer with pink, white or red drumstick flowerheads. Colour depends on variety.
● Maiden pink (*Dianthus deltoides*) is very bright, evergreen, with small red or pink flowers (depends on variety) from early summer through till late summer.
● Euphorbia (*E. myrsinites*) is an evergreen with blue-grey leaves on snaking stems that sprawl over the gravel. Yellowish 'flowers' appear in March and April, but this is really a year-round foliage plant.

● Rock rose (*Helianthemum nummularium*) is another evergreen with greenish or greyish foliage (depends on variety), grown for its prolific flowering. In June and July it is covered with yellow, pink or red flowers 12-25cm (½-1in) across. Dead-heading extends the flowering period.
● Evening primrose (*Oenothera missouriensis*) is a ground-hugging carpeter that has some of the most brilliant and beautiful flowers of all alpines: big yellow saucers that start to appear in June and will go on blooming until the end of summer.
● Polygonum *(P. affine)* is a gradually spreading plant that hugs the ground. Choose the variety 'Donald Lowndes' if you have space for only one. It is compact, the old leaves last until the new ones appear in spring, and the small rose-red pokers that appear in early summer remain attractive for months even when they have died.

The warmth of the dark pink helianthemum and pale pink dianthus is reflected in the colour of these stones (above). The large pieces of gravel deflect the light beautifully.

A succulent, fleshy Euphorbia myrsinites (below) is made more interesting by the stylish arrangement of stones and a border of conifers is given a touch of elegance.

DON'T FORGET!

SAFETY FIRST

- If you have an area of gravel next to a lawn, make sure the gravel does not encroach on to the grass; it could well cause damage to lawnmower blades.
- With smaller children, it is better to choose rounded pea gravel which, unlike gravel chippings, has no sharp edges.

and plants can harmonize. The gravel will form a backdrop for your plants and will help to control weeds.

If the area is large, divide it up into beds with broad gravel paths winding between them. Plant your flowers and shrubs in position and extend a thick layer of gravel from the path over the beds. Provided the gravel is a couple of inches thick over the beds, it will suppress weeds.

As the plants become established and dominate, the gravel links the beds, providing access and an opportunity to explore. You should hoe off the odd weed as it appears or pull it out, or you may prefer to use a suitable weedkiller.

Formal and fancy

Perhaps a sense of design is more important to you than plenty of plants. In this case, gravel is an invaluable material for some types of traditional gardens as well as for more modern, geometric designs.

Elizabethan-style knot gardens, so named for their low hedges which look like knotted ribbons, can look very striking if you introduce areas of various coloured gravels.

Traditionally dwarf box is used in knot gardens but it is both expensive and slow growing. A cheaper and quick-growing alternative, that can be clipped, is cotton lavender (*Santolina chamaecyparisus*). Improvise with other materials, perhaps picking out a pattern with large beach pebbles instead of plants.

Whatever you choose for the outline shape, use at least two colours of gravel to fill in the areas created by the pattern. You could use one colour for the associated paths and others for the infilling.

If you are feeling bold, try a chequerboard pattern or other geometric design, using bricks to define areas, and fill each 'pocket' with a coloured gravel.

Trellis Tricks

Whatever the size of your garden, branch upwards and outwards by introducing trellis – it will enhance its looks and save on space.

A diamond-patterned trellis creates an ideal backdrop for this traditional climbing rose, Rosa 'Galway Bay' (left). The bare wood does not detract from the pretty pink blooms. Because the trellis is attached to wooden battens which are in turn attached to the wall, there is enough room to tie in the roses.

With its diamond, square or rectangular lattice-work design, trellis can perform a number of different functions in the garden. It enables you to branch upwards as well as outwards, training plants to the height you desire. It can be used to mark the boundary of your garden either on its own or on top of a low fence or wall, giving you privacy while allowing light and sunshine to filter through.

Trellis can also be used within the garden as a screen to hide less attractive features such as the compost bin or garden shed, or to give your garden an air of mystery and space by dividing it into separate 'rooms' where a solid screen would have the opposite effect of making it look small and poky. It can also be used against an existing fence, wall or the house itself to support climbing plants or as the framework for a garden feature such as an arbour.

Up and away

Wonderful though trellis is on a grand scale, it really comes into its own when you are trying to make the most of a confined space. By growing just a few well chosen plants upwards and outwards, you can get the maximum display area for the minimum of rootspace.

Trellis comes in a wide variety of forms. Some can be bought as rigid units, while others are sold in a collapsed form ready for expanding and erection in your garden. Plastic-covered mesh types are usually sold from large rolls which are cut to the desired length. Trellis is also available in a wide range of materials.

Made to last

When choosing the type best suited to your garden, you need to consider both its appearance and its durability. It may take several seasons for some climbers to completely smother a trellis while others, including certain roses, may never form a total covering. This type of plant usually looks best against a wooden or painted trellis as this tends to be more attractive than plain metal or plastic.

The main types of trellis fall into distinct categories. Rigid trellis is made either from wood, usually red cedar or softwood, or from plastic-coated steel, and forms square or diamond shapes. This type is readily available from most garden centres and stores. A single piece measures about

Trellis can be used to separate different areas of the garden. Solanum crispum, the Chilean potato tree, scrambles over this trellis (above) bringing it to life with its star-shaped flowers.

Making the most of a confined space, a strip of trellis has been attached diagonally to a wall (below) and a container-grown clematis has been trained up it.

DIAMOND PATTERN TRELLIS

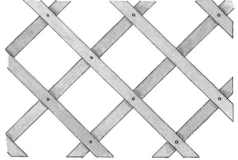

Diamond trellis is not rigid. Attach it to a wall with wooden battens.

SQUARE PATTERN TRELLIS

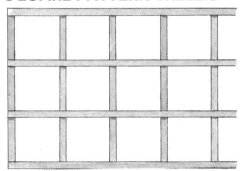

Square trellis is rigid and can be used as a free-standing structure.

3m × 1.2m/6ft × 4ft, so you will probably need a sizeable roof-rack on your car to get it home, or else have it delivered.

You can also get pieces of rigid trellis in a V-shape. These are ideal for supporting a large-flowered clematis, especially when placed on either side of a doorway.

Wooden trellises are easily fixed to walls using screws and proprietary wall fixings. Rigid, plastic-coated steel trellis is

FAN TRELLIS

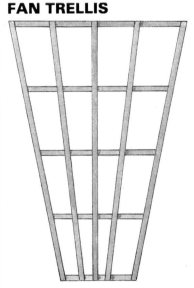

Fan-shaped trellis is ideal for growing climbers in containers.

Fan-shaped trellis can be fixed to a wall as an unusual backdrop for a climber.

PLASTIC COVERED MESH

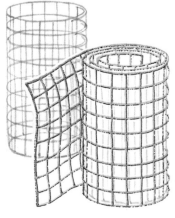

Garden centres cut lengths of mesh from large rolls.

Grow climbers inside a roll of flexible mesh.

Soften the top of a wall with a climber grown on plastic mesh.

93

This open structured square trellis (left) is home-made from lengths of wooden slatting and attached to the wall by battens. The charming miniature climbing rose, Rosa 'Pompon de Paris' has been trained into a fan of blooms.

Fan-shaped trellis is ideal for plants which have little foliage near the base but which burst into leaf a little further up. The trellis (below) encourages the Chilean potato-tree to 'fan' outwards following the line of the attractive brick arch.

Four rectangular pieces of rigid square trellis have been fixed together to form a trellis column (below right). Plants have been chosen for their colour and fragrance. Pure white jasmine, Jasminum officinale, complements the honeysuckle Lonicera × Brownii.

1 Select and mark the position for your trellis, taking into account the plants you wish to grow up it. Drill fixing holes in the trellis.

3 Plant your climber 30cm/1ft away from the wall. Angle the rootball towards wall. Insert a stake and tie the stem in to the trellis.

sold complete with fixings.

Expandable trellis is available in plastic (green or white), western red cedar or softwood and is easily transported when collapsed. It comes in many sizes, some of which can be fixed alongside or under windows. This type of trellis needs to be secured to wooden battens which are in turn fixed to the wall to keep the trellis rigid. It also needs to be about 18mm/¾in from the wall to allow room for the shoots of twining plants to thread themselves through it.

Roll it out

Plastic-covered mesh is sold from large rolls, which are cut to the length you require. It also needs to be attached to wooden battens on walls. The mesh should be stretched between the battens and secured by turning the ends over and under the batten before screwing both batten and mesh firmly to the wall.

This mesh can also be used

RELLIS

2 *Using the trellis as a template, mark drilling holes on the wall. Drill holes in the wall, insert wall plugs and screw trellis in position.*

4 *Once the climber is established, it may look a little bare around the base. Overcome this by under-planting with a display of bedding plants.*

WHAT TO GROW

WALL SHRUBS

Many shrubs smother walls with colourful flowers. Even if they eventually become self-supporting, all benefit at first from the support of a trellis, which enables young shoots to be spaced out and trained as you want them.

- Abutilon (*A. megapotamicum*) has a height and spread of 1.2-1.5m/4-5ft and produces yellow and red flowers (Chinese lanterns) from late spring to autumn. It needs a sheltered position.
- Santa Barbara ceanothus (*Ceanothus impressus*) has a height and spread of 1.5-3m/5-10ft but can be kept low by pruning. It is a slightly tender evergreen shrub with deep blue flowers amid small green leaves in mid- to late spring, and it needs a warm position.
- Fremontia or flannel bush (*Fremontodendron californicum*) has a height of 1.8-3.6m/6-12ft and a spread of 1.2-1.5m/4-5ft. Slightly tender, it is a deciduous or semi-evergreen wall shrub that, although relatively large, can be used to clothe a narrow but high and sunny wall. It has cup-shaped, bright yellow flowers from late spring to autumn.
- Winter-flowering jasmine (*Jasminum nudiflorum*) has a height and spread of 1.2-1.8m/4-6ft. A deciduous wall shrub with semi-double yellow flowers from early winter to spring, it is ideal for shady walls.

PERENNIAL CLIMBERS

There are some lovely perennial climbers for trellises on shady walls.

- Clematis species offer a good range of flower colours, but be careful not to choose a variety that is too vigorous. The height and spread average 1.8-6m/6-20ft, depending on the variety. Flowers appear from late spring to autumn.
- Honeysuckle (*Lonicera periclymenum*) has a height and spread of about 4.5-6m/15-20ft. It has pale yellow flowers with red flushes. Try 'Belgica' for early flowers and 'Serotina' for a spectacular show later in the season.

If your trellis is in a sunny spot, you should choose a climber that likes the sun.

- Jasmine (*Jasminum polyanthum*) has a height and spread of 1.5-2.4m/5-8ft. A slightly tender perennial climber, it has white and pale pink highly scented flowers from spring to early summer.
- Japanese honeysuckle (*Lonicera japonica* 'Aureoreticulata') has a height and spread of 1.8-3m/6-10ft. It has bright green leaves with conspicuous yellow veins.
- Passion flower (*Passiflora caerulea*) has a height and spread of 3.6-6m/12-20ft. Eventually a large climber, it is slightly tender. Restrict it to a trellis around a window. White and blue flowers, are borne from summer to autumn.

ANNUAL CLIMBERS

These are ideal for creating temporary summer colour, with the advantage that you can change the display from year to year. Annuals can easily be grown in large containers on patios with trellis attached to a wall or fence, to provide support.

- Sweet pea (*Lathyrus odoratus*) has a height of 1.2-2.4m/4-8ft. A widely-grown climber, it has many varieties, flowering from summer to autumn.
- Black-eyed Susan (*Thunbergia alata*) grows to 1.2-1.5m/4-5ft high. It is tender and only suitable for growing outdoors in mild areas. Bright yellow flowers with brown centres bloom from summer to autumn.
- Canary creeper (*Tropaeolum peregrinum*) grows to a height of 1.8-3m/6-10ft. It is actually a short-lived perennial, but is invariably grown as an annual. Irregular-shaped yellow flowers are produced from midsummer to autumn.

ROSES

Climbing and rambling roses need support and a wooden trellis is ideal.

- *Pompon de Paris* is a miniature climber with rosy-pink, pompon-like flowers.
- *Rosa ecae* 'Helen Knight' has deep golden flowers.
- 'Étoile de Hollande' has crimson fragrant flowers.

GROWING TIPS

Whatever type of climber you choose, plant it firmly in well-prepared soil, ideally in spring or early summer.

Fork the soil to a depth of about 30cm/12in, adding peat or well-decayed compost. As the soil at the base of a wall tends to dry out rapidly, saturate it a few days before planting the climber. Water the plant a couple of hours before planting.

Put in hole and tease out matted roots from around the sides of the root-ball. Before replacing soil around the roots insert a small bamboo cane to guide the stems up towards the trellis close to the side of the root-ball.

Replace and firm soil around the root-ball, then water the whole area. Later, when the plant is actively growing, lightly fork a general fertilizer into the soil around it.

to form free-standing supports, which are especially effective when used with large-flowered clematis. Cut a 50-60cm/20-24in length of the mesh from a 1.5m/5ft wide roll and form it into a column. Use galvanized wire to secure the ends together, then stand it upright and secure the base to the ground with pegs.

Wooden trellis can also be painted. A green or black trellis will fade into the background while white contrasts with the climber, highlighting foliage and flowers.

Parsley Pots

Tailor-made for a garden in miniature, parsley pots are full of pockets waiting to be packed with the plants of your choice.

their middle width is greater. Crocus pots are smaller – ranging from about 15-20cm/6-8in in height and 7.5-10cm/3-4in width across the top.

Plant selection

Mat-forming plants such as house leeks are ideal subjects for a pocket planter, and so are those that cascade or trail. Plants that grow into small bush shapes, or will grow upright, against the sides of the pot, such as upright rosemary or many thyme varieties are also suitable. Avoid using plants that are wispy and tall: they will look out of proportion with the container.

Remember that the container has many viewing angles. You want to achieve an overall effect, but at the same time, each pocket must look attractive in its own right. The container can also be viewed from above.

Pretty pockets

Think of the planting up of a parsley pot in much the same way as you would plan a planting scheme for a hanging basket. Each individual planting pocket provides its own special part of the finished look of the whole design.

Always combine plants that have similar soil, moisture

Parsley pots are unusual terracotta pots that offer the gardener the chance to grow certain plants intensively in a small space. Strawberry pots and crocus pots are similar in design and, although made and sold with specific plants in mind, you can use them with a variety of plants to create distinctive and eye-catching effects. All have 'pockets' or planting holes around the outside of the pot,

the number of which varies depending on the size of the pot.

Parsley, strawberry or crocus pots can be narrow and cylindrical in shape, rather like an old-fashioned chimney-pot. Most parsley pots are wider in the middle: they bulge at the point where the plants will be closely planted, and vary in depth and width. Some parsley pots are up to 45cm/18in high and up to 30cm/12in wide across the top of the pot, but

Filled with colourful flowers, parsley pots (above) bring instant interest to a patio. These pots are filled with typically popular plants for containers – pelargoniums (geraniums), ivy and fuchsias. In the winter when the more tender plants have to be moved indoors, you can use the pots for early flowering bulbs, near the house so that they can be seen from the windows.

create a rockery garden using alpines and rockery plants? For maximum colour effect select one plant such as yellow alyssum (*A. saxatile* 'Compactum') and put a single plant in each hole. From spring through to midsummer they will bloom brightly, making a cloud of yellow at each planting position. Crown the composition by planting one or two seedlings of another variety of alyssum, such as the double-flowered form 'Flore Pleno', in the top of the container (the number will depend on the size of the pot top).

If you prefer a pink colour scheme, fill the top of the pot with a mat-forming, spring-flowering saxifrage, such as *Saxifraga aizoon* 'Rosea' with its star-like sprays of delicate pink flowers.

Pretty in pink

In some of the holes around the side of the pot, plant *Lewisia cotyledon*, whose white-edged, pink flowers bloom from early summer through to midsummer. In other pockets set a little cushion of sea thrift (*Armeria maritima*) or, for a long flowering period, a rock geranium (*Geranium cinereum*).

Other suitable pink plants include dwarf phlox, (*Phlox subulata*) or a rockery oxalis (*Oxalis adenophylla*). Each of these plants has pretty foliage that will be interesting and attractive even after the flowering season is over.

Tidying up

If they were grown on a rockery, most of these plants would spread up to 45cm/18in. In your planter they may overhang the edge and look a little straggly, but you can trim them off and pot them up to use in other planting schemes, such as a sink garden or rockery. Your container can then be planted up with some summer bedding plants.

This busy Lizzie (above) spills out of its pot in a riot of colour. Mixed crocuses (left) bring an early touch of spring on top of a natural stone wall. They are an ideal size for a parsley pot – larger bulbs, such as daffodils, would be out of proportion. Herbs (below) are also perfect plants for a parsley pot. Regular picking keeps them well shaped and compact but beware of planting mint which can be invasive. This pot includes thyme, curry plant and rue.

and fertilizer preferences. It is no good mixing those that need damp, moist conditions with plants that enjoy dry conditions. Similarly do not combine acid-loving plants with those that prefer a limy soil.

Unglazed terracotta pots are porous, which means that they dry out very quickly. It is therefore advisable to choose plants that can stand dry conditions, such as pelargoniums and petunias. Most of the plants that suit terracotta planting schemes grow well in full sunshine, but to give them a good chance of survival in dry conditions site the pot where it is shaded from the strong heat of the midday sun.

Why not use your planter to

Make sure you clean and disinfect your pot thoroughly before planting it up with something new or you may unknowingly transfer disease to your new plants.

Unglazed terracotta has a rough surface that attracts algae. This enhances the 'natural' appearance of the container but at the same time makes it more difficult to clean. Glazed pots are easier to wash after use but are more expensive to buy than the unglazed kind. The glaze is easily damaged by frost and may begin to chip off.

A riot of colour

Create a summer bedding scheme in miniature using the same plants you would choose for a window box or hanging basket. Grow several colour variations of lobelia to make a frothy cascade of colour from each planting pocket and set a pretty pink or red fuchsia or pelargonium in the top of the pot, and underplant it with two or three variegated, trailing ivy cuttings. The blue-flowered kingfisher daisy (*Felicia bergeriana*) or the perennial pinky-white daisy, *Erigeron karvinskianus* could also be planted in the pockets of your parsley pot, as could dazzling orange and yellow nasturtiums.

If you feel uncertain about mixing and matching colours and flower shapes plant a one-colour and one plant-type scheme. This way you are sure to achieve maximum colour and decorative impact. Trailing fuchsias or ivy-leaf pelargoniums each offer a

A well-established parsley pot (right) is planted with foliage plants whose contrasting texture, colour and shapes are the main source of interest. This is a particularly large parsley pot and the extra space has made it possible to use a shrub in the top without the danger of its roots taking over or competing with the other plants.

PROJECT   **FILLING AND PLANTING UP A PARSLEY POT**

Parsley pots improve almost any area but keep them well watered. In a terracotta container, the compost will dry out more quickly than in a plastic pot.

1 Place a layer of old crocks or stones in the base of your pot to aid drainage.

2 Over the layer of crocks, start to fill your container with a good quality soil-based compost.

4 Cover the roots with compost and move on to the next planting pocket, firming down well. Water.

5 Use the same process as you work up the planting pockets of the pot, filling each hole.

will peep out of the planting pockets on the sides. There are white, pink, light and deep blue varieties of lavender as well as the usual lavender-coloured form.

Other herbs for a fragrant effect include the numerous forms of thyme. Some grow to form compact bushy plants that will hug the pot above the planting pocket, while others grow to form low carpets. Use *Thymus* 'Silver Posie' with its lovely silver and white foliage, *T. vulgaris* 'Aureus', which has bright, golden foliage and *T.* × *citriodorus*, with its lemon-scented leaves.

Mini salad garden

Use your parsley pot to grow all the ingredients you need for a tasty summer salad. Plant up the pockets with parsley, chives and salad burnet, a nasturtium for its edible flowers and a few lettuces, including purple ones and the leafy cut-and-come-again varieties. Plant a compact or even

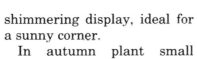

3 *When you reach a pocket, set a plant deep into the hole, anchoring its roots in the pot.*

6 *When you reach the top, set in the top layer of plants and water the container from top and sides.*

shimmering display, ideal for a sunny corner.

In autumn plant small quantities of dwarf spring bulbs in your crocus pot, or into the larger parsley pot. Plant the lovely blue miniature iris, *Iris reticulata*, in the top of your pot, with yellow and white crocus, snowdrops and miniature narcissi in the pockets. This will provide a pretty display throughout the spring months.

Keep the pots in a frost-free place but where the temperatures are low. Wrap them in black plastic and check them every few days to see if the soil has dried out. Remove the plastic and move the pot to a warmer place when the leaves begin to show.

Potted herbs

Lavender is an ideal subject for planting in terracotta parsley pots. It will make an attractive bushy shape in the top of the pot and little clumps

This particularly interesting variation on the usual shape of the parsley pot (above) has been planted with herbs and positioned on a sunny gravel path. There are several unusual pot designs and they can make a very special feature for your garden, so look out for them in your local nursery or garden centre.

Strawberry pots (right), very similar to parsley pots, are a traditional and very suitable way of growing strawberries, even on the tiniest balcony or patio. One danger with strawberries is that the birds will get the fruit before you do, so take care to protect your crop with netting.

In a new garden or on a patio where you want to create instant colour, you can plant up a parsley pot using annuals such as busy Lizzie and begonias. This pot (left) also contains a variety of pot-plants normally used indoors – coleus, spider plant, tradescantia, scented-leaved geranium and baby's tears.

A parsley pot which lives up to its original name and is filled with an abundance of parsley (below) is not only functional in supplying your kitchen with a delicious herb, it makes a very handsome ornament at the side of a formal pond planted with water lilies.

BE CREATIVE

BRIGHT IDEAS

Fill your parsley pot with compost, then push three bamboo canes right down into the pot. Tie the tops together, to form a wigwam. Moisten the compost and sow three sweet pea seeds in every pocket. Sow the top of the pot with up to 15 seeds. Cover with compost and wait for your parsley pot to become a miniature cottage garden.

a trailing form of tomato such as 'Tom Thumb' in the top of the pot, with some basil. If you insert a mini-trellis in the top of your pot you could even succeed in growing a cucumber plant – to complete your salad.

Of course, these pots were really designed for growing a small but useful crop of parsley or strawberries. If you decide to use them for their true purpose, there are a few tips that will help to ensure that you get good results.

Ripe strawberries

When growing strawberries in a traditional terracotta strawberry pot, stand the pot on a tray of pebbles to assist drainage. Ensure that there are drainage holes in the bottom of the pot and place a layer of crocks in the base of the pot, followed by a thin layer of peat. Before adding potting compost, place a roll of fine mesh netting in the pot, to reach up to 15cm/6in from the

rim. The column of netting should be approximately 5cm/2in wide. Fill it to the top with pebbles and cover the top with a small plant pot. Remove the small pot to water the planted pot. This allows the water to reach the pot base and the roots of lower level plants.

A parsley pot can be sown with parsley seeds indoors in early spring or out of doors in late spring. Once the young plants are established, apply a liquid feed every two weeks. In early autumn the parsley should be cut right back to encourage a second lot of healthy new growth. Your pot should keep you supplied with fresh parsley all year round but if you have a bumper crop why not freeze some? Collect it during the summer, wash the leaves and leave them to dry thoroughly. Place them in an airtight container and pop it into the freezer.

A lovely feature

Whatever you grow in your parsley, strawberry or crocus pot, it will make a lovely display. Site your pot in the corner of the lawn, outside the front door or on the patio or balcony, turning it from time to time to ensure that all the plants in it get an equal share of sunlight and rainwater.

Use the pot on its own, as a special feature, or add other terracotta pots of different shapes and sizes to make a pleasing group.

Window Boxes

With a little imagination you can improve the look of your place – from inside and out – by adding a window box of flowers or delightful foliage plants.

The most memorable window boxes are those that appear to cascade with colour and detail, with the container so hidden by foliage and flowers that it looks as if the plants are growing in the air.

To achieve this sort of effect you actually need to exercise restraint. When you first plant it the box will look a little sparse – but give it just a few weeks (and some water and fertilizer) and the plants will develop well.

Lobelia, verbena and trailing pelargoniums are some of the best choices for cascades of colour and texture. For height and spread use petunias or pansies. Tiny blue kingfisher daisies (*Felica bergeriana*) add a delicate touch to such a scheme with their feathery foliage. Trails of silver-leaved helichrysum or variegated ivy will complete the picture.

Whatever you choose to fill your window box, make sure that the box itself is secure on your window sill. If the sill slopes downwards, place two or three wooden wedges under

Twin white window boxes perfectly set off this arrangement of red, white and pink flowers, amid varying shades of green foliage. This late summer display is dominated by the large red floral clusters of pelargoniums. The ivy will provide year-round interest.

box to prevent it slipping.

If your windows open outwards you will need to fix the window box below the window sill. Fix it at least 30cm/12in lower than the sill, so that tall plants will keep their heads when the window is opened.

Materials

Window boxes are available in a range of sizes and different materials.

Terracotta boxes look very attractive but you must be sure that they are frost-proof if winters are severe in your area. They lose water very quickly, so you must be prepared to check regularly that the soil hasn't dried out: in hot weather this may mean twice a day. They are relatively expensive.

Wooden boxes need to be treated against rot. Choose a wood preservative that will not be harmful to the plants in the box. As an extra precaution, line the sides of the box with plastic to prevent water getting into the wood from the inside.

Plastic window boxes are

WINDOW BOX WATCHPOINTS

- Make sure the window box site is accessible so you can plant and maintain it through the year. Once a window box is planted up it will be too heavy to move.
- If you are working from inside the house, lay down newspaper on the floor inside the window and have ready a rubbish bag for any prunings, dead plants or waste compost.
- Always check that the compost is well watered, especially in summer.
- Feed window box plants with a liquid fertilizer during their flowering seasons.
- If there is no one to water your plants when you are on holiday, trail a capillary mat from a bucket of water and bury the other end in the compost. Water will be taken up gradually by the plants. Water the box well before you go away, so that the matting is drenched.

DON'T FORGET!

Crocuses (above) provide early spring colour. Narcissi (below) produce another dash of spring colour in a box that will have looked good all winter, with its mix of evergreens.

the front of the box, to level it. To be absolutely sure that the box is safe you should fix brackets to the wall on either side and one underneath the sill. Each bracket should protrude across the front of the

102

probably the best buy for all-year use. Modern plastics are durable – they don't crack in sunshine and are frost-proof. Once again you must keep an eye on the plants and water them frequently. Drainage holes are usually marked on the base of the box, but you will have to open them using a hand drill. Drip trays are usually bought separately. They hold excess moisture and stop water draining down over your window ledge.

Window box maintenance

To make your window box plants perform well, *you* have to do a bit of work. In the

PLANTING A SPRING BOX

Choose from your favourite spring flowers and create a winter-into-spring window box plan (right). You can achieve garden-like results in the small space of your window box.

1 *Drainage is important, otherwise plants will rot. If you are using a container without drainage holes, such as a plastic trough, bore holes in the base of it.*

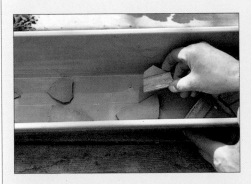

2 *Add a layer of crocks to the bottom of your window box to improve drainage. Broken flowerpots are ideal. Since water passes quickly through them, plants will not be sitting in a pool of stagnant water. Crocks also prevent compost from blocking the drainage holes.*

3 *On top of the crocks add a loamy, soil-based compost. If your window box has no drainage holes, a bulb compost, designed for such situations, can be mixed in with the main compost. For the best results, window boxes should be re-filled each year with fresh compost.*

4 *Before planting up, remove any dead or dying leaves from your plants. Plant ivies in the front of the box to provide different shades and textures of green in winter and daffodils behind for early spring flowering. Water the box well.*

WINDOW BOX THEMES

- **Herb box**: Upright rosemary, sage, thyme and salad burnet offer a good range of colour, shape and flowers.
- **Salad box 1**: 'Tom Thumb' lettuce, clumps of chives and 'Pixie' tomatoes will provide shape, colour and produce.
- **Salad box 2**: Sow cut-and-come-again red and green lettuce in the front of the box and 'Pixie' tomatoes at the back.
- **Spring box**: Plant *Alyssum saxatile* in front to trail over the edge of the box; grape hyacinth bulbs in the next row and dwarf tulips such as *Tulipa greigii* hybrids at the back of the window box.
- **Cascade box**: Trailing fuchsias, ivy-leaved pelargoniums, variegated ground ivy, verbena and trailing lobelia.
- **Up-and-down-box**: For a cascade combined with an upright effect, grow 'Knee-Hi' sweet peas at the back of the box with trailing ivy-leaved pelargoniums in the middle of the box. For trailing foliage use ivy.

ground a plant's roots search for water and food, but in a container the amount of water and nutrient in the soil depends on you. You need to replenish the water constantly, particularly in very hot weather and if the window box is in full sun all day.

Nutrients must be given fairly often. Give your plants a good start by setting them into a loamy, soil-based compost such as John Innes No 2. Peat composts dry out very quickly and have little nutrient material in them. During the growing and flowering season water the box with a liquid fertilizer every fortnight.

When you are planting up the box place a layer of stones or terracotta crocks in the base to improve drainage. The deeper your box, the taller and larger the plants you can grow

in it. For best effects, and if your window sill will hold it, a box 90cm/3ft long x 22cm/9in deep x 25cm/10in wide, is a good size to work with.

A choice of plants

There is a huge variety of plants that you can choose for window box planting schemes. Obviously you can't grow every garden plant in a window box, but you can have a good deal of creative fun choosing the style, colour scheme and shape that your window box collection will have.

With window box gardens you can dress your windows throughout the year with sea-

If your walls are covered with ivy or Virginia creeper, these plants will provide the ideal backdrop for a bright display in a window box. Pink and white petunias have been used (above) to good effect.

A single-colour theme, using various plants, can be very striking. Taking yellow as the theme, this window box (below) has been planted with chrysanthemums, broom (Cytisus) and variegated ivy. Other single-colour arrangements can be equally effective.

sonal favourites that can be removed when they are past their best, replacing them with choice flowers and plants from the following season.

For a permanent framework use evergreen foliage plants and conifers. Variegated ivy, available in a wide range of creamy white and yellow-green combinations, will provide trailing swags of background colour. The ivy trails will also soften and diguise the look of the window box.

Euonymus fortunei 'Emerald Gaiety', an evergreen, upright and bushy shrub, offers cream and green foliage that takes on a rosy tint in autumn. Dwarf conifers come in a range

POSSIBLE PROBLEMS

- Brown or shrivelled leaves are signs of lack of water or of wind burn in winter. In winter, water only sparingly, as the compost will not dry out so quickly.
- Aphids can cause trouble. Spray the plants with soapy water from time to time when you see signs of insect damage.

of silver, grey and golden colours. They add height and shape to a display.

Brightening it up

In between these framework plants you can add winter and spring colour by planting winter-flowering pansies and spring-flowering bulbs and primulas. When the bulbs and spring flowers are finished, remove them and add your favourite summer bedding plants. With such a planting scheme your box always has a basic shape and height, with bright colours each season.

A herb garden in a window box is both useful and attractive. It can be planted up (right) with such herbs as mint, parsley, chives and fennel. Nasturtiums and violas will add colour, while mint and chives can be left to flower.

PLANTS FOR WINDOW BOXES

Flower	Colours	Height	Season
Crocus	yellow, purple cream	8cm/3in	spring
Grape hyacinth (Muscari)	blue, white	18cm/7in	spring
Heathers (Erica carnea)	purple, pink, white	25cm/10in	winter
Pansies	mixed colours	15-20cm/6-8in	summer or winter
Swan river daisy	blue	20-25cm/8-10in	summer/autumn
Busy Lizzie (Impatiens)	red, pinks, striped	15-25cm/6-10in	summer
Tulipa greigii	red, yellow, cream	25cm/10in	late spring
Petunias (dwarf varieties)	pastels, deep reds, blues, doubles	20-30cm/8-12in	summer/autumn
Wallflowers (dwarf varieties)	yellows, orange, dark red	30cm/12in	spring
French marigold (Tagetes patula)	orange, yellow, red, mahogany	15-30cm/6-12in	summer/autumn
Sweet Pea 'Bijou mixed'	mixed	30cm/12in	summer
Trailing plants			
Lobelia	blue, white, mauve	15cm/6in trailing	summer/autumn
Alyssum saxatile	yellow	20cm/8in cascading	spring
Verbena	mixed	25cm/10in trailing	summer/autumn
Ivy-leafed pelargonium	pinks, mauves, some with variegated foliage	25cm/10in trailing foliage	summer/autumn
Nasturtium 'Alaska'	orange, yellow, cream-variegated foliage	30cm/12in trailing	summer/autumn
Nasturtium 'Gleam hybrids'	orange, yellow	30cm/12in trailing	summer/autumn
Foliage plants			
Ivy	green, white, creamy yellow	trailing	all year round
Helichrysum	silvery foliage	trailing	all year in mild areas
Ground ivy	variegated green and white	trailing	all year in mild areas

You can make an all-year herb window box. For the framework of permanent plants, use perennial herbs like sage and thyme. Add nasturtiums and marigolds in summer for colour. (Their petals can be added to summer salads.) Chives and salad burnet also have attractive flowers and their leaves are invaluable in salads.

For an aromatic window box, use lavender or hyssop. Harvest the flowers and leaves of lavender to use in pot pourri or in fragrant drawer bags. You can use the hyssop leaves to add aromatic oils to a bath or as a herbal tea.

Single-colour schemes work well in a window box. In winter use white or purple heathers planted closely like a miniature flowering hedge. Keep them in their individual pots (they like acid soil conditions) and plant bulbs of complementary colours around the heathers. In spring you will then have a fresh look for the window box. Later you can remove the heathers and bulbs and replant the whole box with a summer scheme.

Creating a natural look

Bring a natural look to your spring window box by using alpines and bulbs. *Alyssum saxatile* grows to form a grey carpet and is a perfect companion for a mass of crocuses.

Herbal Window Boxes

Herbs in a window box are handy for cooking but they can be much more than that, providing a fine display of flowers and colourful foliage all year.

If you want a window box that gives an attractive display of colourful flowers and foliage all year round, one filled with herbs is a good choice. It can also perfume the room every time you open the window, and will attract butterflies and provide fresh, flavourful ingredients to liven up your culinary masterpieces.

The size of the box and the fact that you still want to see out of the windows will limit the choice of plants you can grow. Tall species like fennel and tarragon are 'out', as are large bushy evergreens like bay and rosemary. But that still leaves plenty of good compact species.

Do not get carried away by visions of huge bundles of herbs drying decoratively in the rafters though. The amount of herbs you can expect to harvest from a single window box will be limited. You will get enough for weekend cooking, but if you overcut, the appearance of the window box and the health and happiness of the plants in it will certainly suffer.

Planting themes

Many people prefer to create a window box scheme from the widest mixture of herbs possible, chosen to provide a bit of everything. But because space is so limited, it is a good idea to plan a specific planting theme. This makes the box simpler to manage and will provide you with exactly what you want from the display.

If you want lots of herbs to cut for the kitchen, choose fast growing, prolific annuals such as parsley, knotted marjoram,

chervil and varieties of dill and coriander grown for leaf rather than seed.

If scent is the main priority, it pays to have space available indoors in the winter because some of the best subjects, like scented-leaved pelargoniums and pineapple sage, are frost tender. Take cuttings of these in late summer and keep them in trays on a windowsill indoors, replanting them outside in late spring.

For good all year round display, it is essential to include a few evergreens. Try creeping evergreen thymes and perhaps

A window box thickly planted with a range of herbs looks impressive. The varying flower and leaf colours add interest, as do the different growth habits. The plants include sage, nasturtium, lavender and strawberry.

HERB COLLECTIONS

Basils sweet basil (the most commonly seen), bush basil (small leaves, bushy habit), lettuce-leaved basil (large, crinkly leaves used to make Italian pesto sauce), 'Dark Opal' (deep reddish-purple leaves), 'Purple Ruffles' (large, frilly, purplish-red leaves), anise basil (pink flowers, aniseed-scented leaves).

Mints ginger (gold-splashed leaves), eau-de-cologne (perfumed leaves), variegated apple mint (small, round, hairy, silver-variegated leaves), spearmint (the best for mint sauce), peppermint (dark leaves, good for mint tea).

Oriental herbs perilla (used in Japanese cookery with bean curd), kemangie (lemon basil used in Indonesian cookery), coriander (leaves used in Indian cookery), Japanese parsley (celery/parsley flavour), Chinese chives (robust version of normal chives).

Thymes (*Thymus* species) Creeping evergreen: *T. serpyllum coccineus* . 'Major', *T.s.* 'Minimus' and *T.s.* 'Minus' or 'Minor'. Scented, upright: *T. fragrantissimus* (orange thyme), *T. × citriodorus* (lemon thyme), *T. herba-barona* (caraway scented). Woolly-leaved, creeping: *T. lanuginosus*.

The pale pink flowers and variegated leaves of Thymus vulgaris *'Silver Posie' (above) look good on their own or as part of a larger collection of thymes.*

*Ginger mint (*Mentha × gentilis *'Variegata') has golden-yellow leaf veins (left). It has a pungent aroma.*

Three sages and two marjorams (below) provide a good contrast in foliage colours.

a tricolor sage, prostrate rosemary and dwarf lavender. These will need an annual tidy with scissors after flowering to keep them small and shapely.

You could also add a few annual flowers for extra colour in summer. Brightly coloured salvia or French marigolds team up well with red-leaved basil 'Dark Opal' (itself an annual). Or use subtler flowers like night-scented stock for scent. Sow the flower seeds directly into the box.

Single groups

If you have a special interest in a particular group of herbs, such as mints, thymes, basil or exotic oriental herbs, you can set up the window box to provide ideal conditions for them.

Mint, for instance, soon swamps other herbs in a mixed window box. By growing it alone you avoid this problem. It also takes much of the nourishment packed into the potting compost.

In a window box it needs more feeding and watering than other herbs. Tip mint out every spring, divide the plants and replace them in fresh soil-based compost.

Basils and oriental herbs, on the other hand, need very warm sheltered conditions and a dryish soil to do well.

Although most herbs prefer a warm, sunny site, if you only have a cold, shady one available you can still have a herbal

window box. It will be slightly unconventional but still effective. Plant up some old fashioned medicinal herbs, such as woodruff, bugle and lady's mantle. Since many of these are British native species, they also make a good 'ecological' window box.

And if space permits, why not continue the herbal theme into nearby containers at ground level? Matching window boxes and troughs, with similar planting schemes, can create a very nice rural atmosphere in even the tiniest of town courtyards.

The choice of box

Where possible choose a good sized, deep window box. Timber ones should be treated inside and out with wood preservative and allowed to dry thoroughly before planting. Line them with polythene to extend their life further.

Terracotta window boxes should be frost resistant; they are in any case heavy and need strong supports. Plastic window boxes should be of top quality, as cheap plastics become brittle after prolonged exposure to sunlight.

The best site for herbal window boxes is in plenty of sun, sheltered from strong winds. Given sun for less than half the day the plants will grow but will be rather leggy. In permanent shade it is vital to choose shade-tolerant species.

Buying herbs

Many herbs are readily available in garden centres. Less common varieties are available from specialist nurseries and herb farms. Check who stocks particular varieties in the current edition of a 'plant finder' directory.

Buy small plants in 8.5cm/ 3½in pots if you can. The huge pots of herbs now being sold for garden planting are too big for window box use. Make sure herb plants are fairly bushy, a good fresh green colour, and free from any obvious signs of pests or diseases.

Most herbs can be raised from seed provided you have the space; sow in small pots on a warm window-sill indoors, then transplant to the window box. Specialist seed firms supply seeds for unusual plants such as oriental herbs.

Planting

Drill three or four drainage holes in the base of the window box if they are not already present. Cover these with concave pieces of broken clay flowerpot or with stones to prevent the compost running out through them.

A beautifully designed window box with examples of many species of herbs (top). Because the plants are generously spaced, the differences in height and the varied leaf colours and shapes can be clearly seen. A mulch on the surface keeps down weeds and enhances the look.

The leaves of variegated apple mint (above) not only look good, they also smell of apples.

Place a 2.5cm/1in layer of coarse gravel in the base of the window box if extra drainage is necessary. Then fill with a good quality John Innes (soil based) potting compost.

Pot-grown perennial herbs can be planted at any time of year, except during bad weather. Annuals are best planted in late spring or early summer, as soon as the risk of damaging frosts is past.

Some annuals which are grown for leaf production, such as chervil, basil and varieties of dill and coriander, are notoriously short-lived. You will need to re-sow seeds or replace with new plants several times during the season for continuity of cutting.

Aftercare

Check window boxes regularly to see if they need watering. Herbs will not need feeding for six to eight weeks after planting, since the compost will provide all they need. From then on, feed once a week in summer with a general purpose liquid plant feed. No feeding is necessary from mid-autumn until mid-spring.

Window boxes of annual herbs are best remade every year in spring, just before planting time. Replace the old compost with fresh material.

Boxes of mainly perennial herbs can be left for two or three years, until the plants become overgrown and need dividing or replacing with younger, neater looking specimens. Again, the best time to replant is mid to late spring.

Pineapple sage (Salvia rutilans) has neater leaves than most sages. It looks good (above) but has no culinary uses. The leaves, however, do smell of pineapple when crushed. The plant has red flowers.

The rich purple leaves of perilla (below) contrast strongly with a collection of green-leaved herbs. The leaves have a spicy smell when bruised. This is Perilla frutescens *'Atropurpurea'.*

Winter Window Boxes

Cold weather need not bring your window box displays to an end. Arrangements of colourful foliage and flowers will brighten up winter window-sills.

TIMING PLANTING

There is a temptation to keep summer-flowering plants in place while they are still colourful. However, a winter box should be planted up by mid-autumn, otherwise the contents have little time to become established before the cold weather arrives.

There are a number of ways of achieving successful winter displays. One of the simplest is to use box liners that you can slip in and out of your window box. These liners, usually made of recycled cellulose, allow you to prepare an attractive arrangement of plants in advance.

You can plant up box liners with winter-flowering bulbs, pansies or primulas. As soon as summer plants are past their best they can be removed and can be replaced by the already planted and partially established winter containers. Use two or three to fill a box; a larger size would be too heavy to move when planted up.

At the end of the flowering season the liners can be placed in a less obvious part of the garden to allow bulb foliage to die back naturally.

An arrangement of evergreens (above), enlivened by the deep pink blooms of cyclamen. The small shrub with leaves dotted yellow is spotted laurel (Aucuba japonica), a versatile permanent plant for window boxes. Grow both male and female plants if you want red berries from autumn to spring. There are a number of varieties.

Another option is to include in your window box some permanent plants that look good the whole year round.

Permanent framework

A design based around evergreens allows you to fill in the spaces between them each season with appropriate colourful flowers. Heathers, ivies and miniature conifers and evergreen shrubs are ideal permanent plants.

Foliage need never be dull. Conifers and heathers have foliage in shades of green or in red, gold or bronze. Many evergreen shrubs and ivies have colourful variegated leaves.

Conifers come in a wide var-

iety of shapes, from slim spires to globes. Some form squat cushions and there are ground-covering forms that hang over box edges. Together with low, spreading heathers and trailing, evergreen creepers, there is no shortage of shapes to choose from.

Creating a skeleton design from evergreens keeps work and expense to a minimum.

Evergreens in pots

If you prefer to remove all the summer plants and replace them at the onset of winter, grow a few evergreens in pots. Sink them into the compost in your box and plant bulbs and flowering plants around them.

A simple design (above left) of upright blue-green conifers with variegated Euonymus fortunei *and ivy. If you have little or no window-sill, a window box should be attached securely to the wall just below the window.*

The window box itself can add a splash of colour (above right) to brighten up a window-sill. This one has a black steel framework with red ceramic tiles.

The white flowers of heather and viola (below) complement a cream and green hebe and contrast well with the dark greens of a cypress and ivy.

Working to a shape creates the best effect. If the view from your window is pleasing use a swag arrangement to provide a decorative frame.

Designing a shape

Suitable plants for the box ends would be two slim, column-shaped conifers, such as young *Chamaecyparis lawsoniana* 'Elwoodii', which has attractive grey-green foliage.

A compact, globe-shaped *Cryptomeria japonica* 'Compressa', which has green foliage, tinted red-purple in winter, could go next. Plant winter-flowering heathers in the centre, with ivy or periwinkle trailing over the edge.

If you prefer a less symmetrical design, place two tall, slim conifers at one end. *Picea glauca albertina* 'Conica', for

FIRM FIXINGS

Winter winds make it especially important that boxes are securely fixed. Use wall plugs and screws to fix brackets to the wall, and where possible, screw the brackets to the base of the box. For added safety screw a hook to the wall either side of the window and fix large screw eyes in both ends of the box. Run thick wire or a chain between each hook and screw eye.

SAFETY FIRST

instance, makes a compact green pyramid. Then add smaller, dome-shaped types towards the centre and include one medium-sized spherical conifer at the opposite end.

Partially hide an ugly view with variegated ivy trained on wires fixed across the lower half of the window. In summer, add flowering climbers like nasturtiums or the unusual canary creeper (*Tropaeolum peregrinum*).

If you want to use tall plants in a box without obstructing the view, you should fix the box to the wall below sill level.

Colour schemes

As winter-flowering window box plants are seen in the main from inside the house they look most effective if they tie in with the room's decoration. Alternatively, go for a

An attractive terracotta box (right) sets off the cascading stems of a variegated ivy. White violas add floral appeal.

contrast by choosing sunny colours against the background of a room with a cool white, green or blue interior.

A golden scheme can be based around the gold-tinted conifers shown in the chart. Add yellow-flushed ivies like *Hedera helix* 'Goldheart', which has yellow centres to its leaves, or *H. h.* 'Buttercup',

SLOW-GROWING CONIFERS

Type and habit	Foliage colour	Approx maximum size
Ground cover forms		
Juniperus chinensis 'Pfitzerana Aurea'. Low, prostrate form	golden	150cm/60in spread
J. conferta conferta. Carpeter	silver on underside	90cm/36in spread
J. squamata 'Blue Star'. Forms compact mound	silvery blue	60cm/24in spread
Pyramid forms		
Chamaecyparis obtusa 'Nana Aurea'. Foliage in twisted whorls	golden	60cm/24in height
C. pisifera 'Plumosa Pygmaea'. Cone-shaped bush	golden	90cm/36in height
Juniperus communis 'Compressa'. Compact spire shape	grey-green	45cm/18in height
Picea glauca 'Nana'. Bush shape	grey-blue	90cm/36in height
Thuja occidentalis 'Rheingold'. Fine, feathery foliage	soft gold turning bronze in winter	100cm/40in height
Globe-shaped forms		
Chamaecyparis pisifera 'Compacta Variegata'. Low bun shape	golden	60cm/24in height
Thuja occidentalis 'Globosa'. Small dense globe	strong green	45cm/18in height
T. orientalis 'Aurea Nana'. Egg-shaped bush	bright gold-green turning bronze in winter	60cm/24in height
T. orientalis 'Minima Glauca'. Miniature globe	blue-green	30cm/12in height
T. orientalis 'Rosedalis'. Upright oval	summer:green/winter: purple/spring: yellow	60cm/24in height

NOTE: Most of these conifers will only grow 1-2cm/½-1in per year.

which has new leaves of bright yellow that soften to pale green later.

Choose bulbs like winter aconite (*Eranthis hyemalis*) which, in late winter, has buttercup-coloured flowers surrounded by a ruff of green bracts. Or you could plant the yellow, early-spring-flowering crocus, *Crocus chrysanthus* 'E.A. Bowles'.

For a silver and white scheme pick variegated *Euonymus fortunei* 'Silver Queen', a shrub with green leaves edged in creamy white. Add white heathers, particularly the varieties of *Erica herbacea* (also sold as *E. carnea*). *E. h.* 'Cecilia M. Beale' blooms from early winter, while *E. h.* 'Springwood White' flowers vigorously from late winter.

Among the many ivies go for *Hedera helix* 'Silver Queen' with its green and silver leaves, or, in a sheltered situation, *H. h.* 'Eva' which has delightfully small, grey-green

Skimmias are hardy, evergreen shrubs, ideal for winter window boxes. They are usually grown for their bright clusters of red berries (above). One variety has red-brown flower buds (top right) in autumn and winter, which add subtle variety to this box of evergreens and colourful cyclamens, though this type of cyclamen is not frost-hardy.

leaves edged with cream.

There is little to rival the heart-warming emergence of snowdrops. *Galanthus elwesii* has large flowers that appear in late winter.

A blue and pink scheme could include the blue-green conifers and the ivy *H. helix* 'Tricolor', which has white-bordered leaves that turn a deep pink in autumn.

Several varieties of frost hardy cyclamen flower in autumn, winter or early spring.

The bright pink flowers of *Cyclamen coum*, for instance, appear in early winter. There are also many different pink heathers to choose from.

Winter care

As most window boxes are sheltered from the rain by the house wall, they will need watering often, even in winter. Conifers, in particular, require moist conditions, as do pansies and primulas. If frost is expected, do not water until conditions turn warmer.

Winter-flowering plants need feeding but for most plants winter is a time of rest. Feed the plants in your winter box once, a few weeks after planting, then just once or twice in spring.

Extreme cold winds can damage the foliage of even hardy plants. It is worth protecting your box in severe frost or snow with a covering of sacking. House walls offer some protection. In extreme cold, the city dweller, surrounded by warm buildings, has the advantage over those living in the country.

Creating an Arbour

An arbour is a lovely, leafy hideaway where you can talk with a friend or sit in peace away from the world, surrounded by wafts of natural scent.

An arbour is a private place, a seat surrounded by foliage that excludes the outside world. Traditionally, they have been used for romantic encounters and political intrigue. In a small, modern garden, the arbour comes into its own as somewhere you can sit and read, have tea, or just enjoy the plants.

The simplest kind of arbour is a small sitting place, enclosed on three sides by trees and shrubs or by trellises covered with plants. It has no top and is open to the sky.

You should aim to create a snug space where no more than four adults can sit. Ar-

A lovely wooden arbour (left) with trelliswork sides, a paved floor and a comfortable wooden bench. A honeysuckle, Lonicera × americana, covers the roof and Rosa 'Iceberg' (seen in detail below) is growing up the trellises.

Japanese wisteria (Wisteria floribunda 'Macrobotrys') will cover pergolas and trellises with its long lilac blooms in early summer (above).

bours are not designed for deckchairs or for sprawling. They are for more decorous sitting, so your four people will not take up much room. An internal area of one to two square metres/yards is enough.

Hedging

The long-term way of making this kind of arbour is to make it part of a hedge. As long as it is a non-prickly hedge it does not matter what it is made of as long as it will prune neatly. Yew is ideal, but very slow, while western red cedar (*Thuja plicata*), another conifer, is much faster growing and responds well to trimming.

Whatever you use should be evergreen (so use oval-leaved privet, not the common one that loses its leaves in winter) and should be rigid in habit.

The evergreen honeysuckle *Lonicera nitida* is useless, as it has to be staked at heights over 1.2m/4ft.

If you cannot wait for hedge plants to grow up, you can use trellis and grow climbers over it. There is nothing to stop you choosing modern materials, but rustic trellis made from larch poles is much better and looks entirely natural when it is covered in plants.

A hedging arbour has a forlorn appearance if you try to make it free-standing. It needs to be part of an internal or boundary hedge, even if it is only a short one. A trellis arbour, however, can be either part of a longer trellis or can stand on its own.

Both types will form a significant vertical feature in the garden, as the height of the

smallest arbour will need to be 2m/6½ft (heads bobbing up and down in an arbour look positively silly).

Clematis and rambling roses are perfect for growing over hedge arbours; honeysuckles and ornamental vines can be allowed to twine and scramble over trellis.

Bowers

Roofed arbours – often called bowers – are more intimate than simple ones and usually have a wide doorway, rather than an entirely open side. They are generally designed for two people sitting side by side or across a corner and, traditionally, their width exceeds their depth.

They were made in several ways, the quickest and easiest of which was to grow trees –

usually hornbeam – in a two-thirds circle and fuse them together at the top by bending and grafting when they had grown tall enough. This made a leafy, covered arbour but it was rather large and leaked.

The best roofed arbours for small gardens are made with hedging plants trained on metal frames with hooped tops. The plants take quite a long time to grow and need re-

Wooden trelliswork arbours (above) can be extremely decorative in their own right, especially early in the year before they are clad with climbing plants. The oriental style of this one is emphasized by an eye-shaped patch of gravel in front of it. Fine-stemmed climbers with striking blooms, such as clematis and sweet pea, will complement the delicate design without smothering it.

It is hard to beat the rich colours of clematis flowers (above right). This is Clematis viticella 'Abundance', a late-flowering species which is fully hardy.

This arbour (right), set against a fence, is covered with Russian vine (Polygonum baldschuanicum). This rampant, twining climber very quickly provides thick cover and must be regularly cut back into shape. It flowers in late summer and autumn.

HEDGE CARE

Hedging arbours should be clipped twice a year, preferably in late spring and late summer. All signs of disease and attacks by pests should be taken seriously, as years of work can be destroyed quite quickly. At the first sign of a problem, spray with a systemic insecticide or systemic fungicide. Spray flowers after dusk or before sunrise to avoid damage to bees.

A wooden arbour should be treated with a wood preservative (right) when it is first erected and then given regular coats in subsequent years. Any wooden furniture should be similarly treated to prolong its life. The woodwork will soon become weathered and blend naturally with its surroundings, as can be seen in the picture of a similar arbour on page 114. Siting an arbour against a wall like this provides a solid barrier against the wind.

Trachelospermum jasminoides, which is commonly called star jasmine or Confederate jasmine (below), is a woody-stemmed, evergreen, twining climber that can be grown on trellises, pergolas and even on hedging arbours. It has very fragrant, white flowers in summer, followed by pairs of pods, and the plant is frost hardy.

DON'T FORGET!

PROTECTING WOOD

Treat wooden trellis with a copper-based preservative, preferably of a brown shade rather than green. Leave for a month before introducing plants. Creosote is a splendid preservative but may damage plants for up to six months.

Do not concrete wooden trellis posts into the ground; they just rot all the quicker. It is much better to buy metal 'feet' from a garden centre.

gular clipping but are delightful. In a formal setting you need only give them 'wings' of hedge on either side.

An open trellis arbour can be provided with a roof. It is best left with a fully open side, as it will appear dank if you try to copy the doorway style. A roofed hedging arbour is a refuge from showers, whereas a trelliswork one is not.

One end of a pergola can be made into an arbour using trelliswork of any kind. Just enclose the last 1m/3ft or so of its length. Pergolas are supposed to be thoroughfares, leading from one place to another, but if yours does not, it can lead to your arbour.

Flooring

Wherever you make your arbour, you should give it a proper floor. Soil and grass will just wear away and cover your shoes alternately with dust and mud. The floor should extend some way out of the arbour, too, to integrate it with the rest of the garden and allow you to sweep leaves out of it more easily.

Simple bricks or small pavers are ideal, laid either conventionally or in a pattern. Large slabs are not always a good idea; they can look out of scale. Keep your flooring free of slippery algae.

Where you construct your arbour is a matter of personal

preference. You may prefer to have it in a corner, or as a niche in the boundary hedge, or even as the centrepiece of the whole garden, opening on to a circle of paving with a fountain in the middle. Some people like to see the whole garden from the arbour; others prefer it to be a completely private hideaway.

Whatever you do, choose a sunny place. Nothing is worse than an arbour that is wet and dark, over which no plants will grow. Neither you nor anyone else will want to sit in it.

Seating

Comfortable seating is important. Stone is not recommended; it looks good but most people stay for five minutes and then move on. Slatted timber garden seating, properly shaped and with a good back is by far the best.

Start, then, with your seating. Decide roughly what size you want your arbour to be, see what seating is on the market, and then design your arbour to fit around it.

The green-painted metal framework of this arbour (right) has almost disappeared beneath a mass of honeysuckle and Artemisia arborescens. This silvery-leaved artemisia from southern Europe can grow to 1.8m/6ft in a sunny site, but it is not reliably hardy and may succumb to harsh winters in cold areas. It goes well with the scented flowers of the taller, climbing honeysuckle because its delicate, feathery foliage is aromatic.

The dividing line between an arbour, a bower and a pavilion or summer-house is a matter of debate. This white, trellised, metalwork structure (below) is a free-standing centrepiece which is attractive on its own but could be readily enhanced by the addition of plants. Climbers could be grown up the pillars and across the roof, and window boxes could be hung from its sides. There are many ready-made designs on the market.

Wall-trained Fruit Trees

Turn your fences and walls into a mini-orchard. Planted with fan, cordon or espalier-trained fruit trees, they make attractive – and productive – garden features.

Conventional fruit trees, even those on modern dwarfing rootstocks, take up too much space for most small gardens. Think how much better a flat tree would fit in.

Wall-trained trees are just that. They are trained flush to the wall, with no branches sticking out to obstruct a path, or get in the way in the middle of a lawn or flower bed.

If you do not have a spare wall, then a fence – or even a row of 2m/6ft posts with four horizontal wires stretched between them – will provide a good, sturdy support.

Cordon and espalier trees, trained on posts and wires, can be used to create 'fruiting hedges'. These are a handy way to divide a vegetable garden from the main ornamental garden, or to give height to the back of a border. But remember to leave a path for ease of pruning and picking.

The benefits

Wall-trained fruit trees may not give as much fruit as a full-sized conventional tree, but

A mature fan-trained apple tree graces an old stone garden wall. New shoots have been tied to inconspicuous wires running the length of the wall. The tree is fruiting heavily and the bulk of the apples can be picked from the ground.

Fan trees are grown on vigorous rootstocks. The branches radiate out.

Espalier trees have a central stem and symmetrical, parallel branches.

Cordon trees take the least space with their short fruit spurs.

the trained tree is more compact. You actually get more fruit per square metre/yard from trained trees, because the method of pruning encourages the production of fruit buds on clusters of twigs.

The other bonus with trained fruit is that, since it takes up less space, you have room to grow a bigger range of varieties. So, in place of a single apple tree, you could grow a fan-trained peach, half a dozen different cordon-trained apples, with fruit ripening from late summer onwards, and a couple of cordon pears.

Apart from the obvious benefit, this also improves pollination. A single tree in a small garden may not have a suitable pollinator tree growing nearby, and will only give a poor crop – or none at all – despite flowering well. By growing several varieties, the chances of good pollination, and therefore good crops, are obviously far better.

Choosing tree shapes

The three basic shapes for wall-trained fruit trees are fans, cordons or espaliers.

Cordons are the most compact if space is really limited. They are also the fastest to start cropping since it does not take long to form their shape.

Fans and espaliers are more decorative, but take longer to train into shape initially. For this reason, it is a good idea to

A 'Conference' pear tree trained as an espalier along a wooden fence (above).

Young apple trees in blossom (left). They are cordon-trained.

Fine 'James Grieve' apples on a cordon (right). This is a good eating apple.

A 'Stella' cherry (below), fan-trained on a wattle fence. The branches are being trained along bamboo canes.

buy them already trained (when they start cropping within a year or two), but plants will be more expensive.

Cordons

Cordons have a single stem, usually growing on the slant, from which fruit spurs (short branching clusters of twigs) grow, and carry the crop.

Cordon training is mostly used for apples and pears growing on moderately dwarfing rootstocks.

Cordon trees can be bought already trained, and should start cropping lightly the year after planting. Pruning is done in midsummer.

The idea is to trim the new shoots growing from the fruiting spurs back to 2.5-5cm/1-2in of their base. This is just above the point where the clusters of fruit are developing. (See project box).

You can save a few pounds by training your own cordons. It is quite easy, and they take two years to start cropping. (See project box).

Espaliers

Espalier training is generally used for apples and pears. Espaliers have a single upright trunk from which two or maybe three pairs of branches grow opposite each other, spaced 60cm/2ft or so apart, at right angles to the trunk.

Each branch is rather like a cordon tree, but it grows horizontally. It has fruiting spurs along its length like a cordon, and each branch is pruned in exactly the same way as a complete cordon tree.

Forming the shape of an espalier takes several years and requires regular attention. It is best to buy young

1 Fix four horizontal wires spaced 45cm/18in apart to a wall, fence or row of posts.
2 Buy 1-2 year old maiden trees in winter. Plant them 75cm/30in apart, at an angle of 45 degrees to the ground.
3 Support each trunk with a 2.4m/8ft cane pushed into the ground for 30cm/1ft. Tie the trunk at intervals of 30-45cm/12-18in.
4 Cut back any laterals (sideshoots) to 10cm/4in from the trunk when you plant the tree.

THE FIRST YEAR

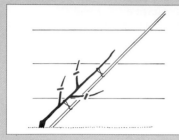

5 In spring, remove any flowers that appear, to allow the tree to establish and develop its shape.
6 'Summer prune' in midsummer. Cut back any new laterals to 10cm/4in as before, and shorten sublaterals (sideshoots arising from existing sideshoots) to 2.5-5cm/1-2in from their base, just above the clusters of young, developing fruit.
7 When the leaves fall, cut back all the new growth that has appeared since summer pruning to 2.5cm/1in from its base, again cutting just above a bud. This will build up lots of fruiting spurs which will carry the crop.

FOLLOWING YEARS

8 In second spring, remove premature flowers, leaving basal rosettes, to discourage early fruiting. Summer prune each year. When the fruiting spurs become densely branched, thin them out in winter by removing weak growths, leaving strong, well-spaced shoots.

ready-trained trees from a nursery. These should start fruiting the second summer after planting.

If space is short, you can buy espalier trees in which each branch is a separate variety; a 'family' tree. You can get family apple trees and family pears – but not on the same tree.

A family tree can be very useful if you only have room for one wall-tree, as the varieties used are carefully chosen to cross-pollinate each other. Between them they will produce a succession of fruit, ripening over a long period.

Fans
Fan-trained trees have their branches radiating out in a traditional fan shape from the base of the plant.

This form of training needs a fairly vigorous plant. It is commonly used for fruit for which no really dwarfing rootstocks are as yet available. These include plums, peaches, nectarines, apricots, almonds and cherries.

Since these fruits need warmth to ripen properly, they do best grown against a south-facing wall or fence. Except in very mild, sheltered areas, they do not do well grown on posts and wires situated out in the open.

Growing the trees against a wall or fence also makes it much easier to protect them from birds. Just nail a batten along the top of the wall, tack bird netting to it and drape it down over the trees as the fruit starts to ripen.

Fan-trained 'Rochester' peaches protected by netting from the birds (above). The netting has been fixed to the top of the fence and draped down.

Tree nurseries train fruit trees so that gardeners can buy them ready-trained. These pear trees (left) are being trained as cordons.

The 'Morello' cherry (below) flowers late and is suitable for a north wall. This variety is self-fertile.

Some people even build a permanent wooden framework over which nets can be draped for the fruiting season.

Like espaliers, training a fan from scratch takes several years and is quite complicated. It is far better to buy a young tree whose basic shape has already been formed.

Routine pruning is then keeping it in shape, and periodically renewing old fruiting branches with young vigorous shoots. (See box).

Any fairly sheltered site can be used for trained fruit, provided the soil is fertile and not waterlogged in winter or strongly acid or alkaline.

Orientation

A south- or west-facing wall is really best for most fruit. East-facing walls should be avoided since fruit flowers early in the season when there is a risk of late frosts. If the early morning sun shines directly onto frozen flowers they are killed and the crop is lost for that year. North-facing walls can however be used to grow 'Morello' (cooking) cherries.

ROUTINE PRUNING OF FAN TREES

Late winter – cut back the main shoots that make up the 'ribs' of the fan by one third. Prune to just above a bud.
Bud-burst – in spring, when growth buds start to develop, prune back to the base any sideshoots that are growing in towards the wall or outwards over the path.
Summer – tie new shoots in to the wall (using wall nails, or use string to tie them to trellis). The idea is to fill in any gaps that may have developed in the fan pattern.
Replacing old branches – after several years, when the wall is completely covered with branches, start replacing a few of the oldest branches with vigorous young shoots.

Choose one strong shoot growing from the base of each of the branches to be replaced and mark it with a piece of coloured ribbon.

After the fruit have been picked (in the case of peaches, apricots and nectarines), or in winter (plums) or when the buds start to burst in spring (cherries), prune the old fruited shoot back to just above the shoot you have left. Then tie the new shoot into place.

123

Container Rhododendrons and Azaleas

The many varieties of rhododendron and azalea can flower in winter, spring or summer. Dramatic when in bloom, they always look good in containers.

Have you ever wished your display of plants in pots and containers would go on right through the year, with at least something green to look at during the depths of winter?

One way of achieving this is to grow rhododendrons or azaleas in containers. You can then have rich colourful flowers in summer, and some good evergreen foliage through the winter. They make a perfect choice for containers in town gardens, and if you live on limy soil, either in town or country, this may be the only easy way for you to grow these lime-hating but spectactularly beautiful plants.

Remember that azaleas are just a particular kind of rhododendron. They are generally more delicate in appearance, with smaller flowers, and are often deciduous or semi-evergreen, but they can be grown in just the same way as the usually larger, evergreen rhododendrons.

Good in pots

Rhododendrons are ideally suited to life in containers. They have attractive foliage all the year, some with small rounded leaves and others with long glossy ones. They make an even, domed shape which is very pleasing in a container, as is the more bowl-

Azaleas (right) and rhododendrons make stunning container displays and are easy to care for.

Rhododendron 'Cowslip' (above) is a popular and easily available variety, with creamy-yellow flowers in early to mid spring.

The dramatic, glowing red blooms of R. 'Britannia' (right) have made it a gardener's favourite. Tough and wind-resistant, it is particularly well-suited to a container.

The imperial colour of R. 'Purple Splendour' (below) is unusual to find among rhododendrons. This variety, with attractive frilled flowers and a prominent black ray in the throat, flowers in late spring and early summer.

shaped outline of the rather smaller azaleas.

They all have shallow roots which can be easily accommodated in a pot, and there is no tap-root. They are not hungry plants and require little in the way of feeding.

There are, however, one or two aspects of life in a pot which rhododendrons do not relish. They need cool, shady soil, and do not like dry soil and heat around their roots.

Although they like a lot of water, they hate being water-logged. Not all rhododendrons are hardy when their roots are in a container that is above the ground and exposed to the frost. Some extra protection is often a good idea.

Buying your plants

Generally speaking, the tougher hybrid rhododendrons are most suitable for growing in containers.

The more tender species are better avoided, however elegant they may be.

Look for low densely-foliaged specimens with no hint of yellow in the leaves. You can choose root-balled or

pot-grown plants.

It makes sense to buy your plants in spring when they will be ready to plant out in the new compost of a container. Pot-grown specimens can be planted into containers any time during the summer. If you buy a rhododendron in

125

FEEDING

Rhododendrons and azaleas are not hungry plants and positively resent large doses of fertilizer. As long as they look healthy and flower well, resist the temptation to feed them regularly.

The best type of nourishment for a rhododendron is a top dressing of leaf mould in the spring, preferably enriched with a little bone meal.

Treating the plants with Sequestrene or a similar plant 'tonic' from time to time (but do not overdo this) will ensure that they get the trace elements, such as iron, that are necessary to healthy growth.

winter, keep the plant in its existing pot, or in the ground, until you put it into its container in the spring.

Composts

Ordinary potting compost — even peat-based ones — contain too much lime for most rhododendrons. You need to buy ericaceous compost, which is formulated especially for acid-loving plants like rhododendrons and heathers.

Work a little extra grit into the compost to keep it free-draining, and make the compost at the bottom of the pot very gritty. The grit, of course, must not be limestone. Use a layer of broken clay pots to cover the holes in the bottom of the container.

Leaf mould makes an excellent alternative to ericaceous compost, if you can get it, and should also be mixed with grit.

When planting your rhododendron, make sure you leave the soil level 4-5cm/1½-2in below the rim of the pot to allow for generous watering.

Tubs

In choosing containers for rhododendrons, look for ones which are wider than they are high. A tub made from half a barrel is about right, although it would be far too big as a first pot for most new rhododendrons. However, any large wooden, stone, concrete or terracotta container makes a good home for these plants.

Plastic pots will do for rhododendrons, but they are not as good as terracotta or other tubs, even if they retain the moisture better.

Growing on

Keep your containerized rhododendrons in a bright, sunny place during the summer, but one which is not too hot.

The tender indoor azaleas (*Rhododendron simsii*) can of course be plunged, in their pots, into garden soil for the summer in half shade, but must be brought indoors again before the autumn.

Most rhododendrons and azaleas make a good, even shape of their own accord, but it may be necessary on occasion to pinch out a tip or two, to make the plant bush out.

A fairly large and sturdy terracotta pot (left) is an ideal home for a container-grown rhododendron. Since a pot of this size and weight is not easy to move, choose a sunny but sheltered spot for the plant, to provide winter protection.

R. yakushimanum (right) is one of the best rhododendrons for containers, growing to a dome-shaped height of about 90cm/36in. Its pretty flowers are starkly white when open but deep pink in bud.

The Kurume hybrid azalea 'Amoenum' (below right), with striking magenta-pink flowers appearing in spring, is evergreen, thus providing winter interest.

R. 'Daviesii' (below), a deciduous Ghent azalea, is notable for its fragrant, creamy-white and yellow blotched flowers.

Plants should be potted on every two or tree years. A good guide is the spread of the plant's foliage. When this is almost twice the width of the pot, then it is time to re-pot.

Like garden rhododendrons, most container-grown plants are not easily damaged by cold or frost. However, most will benefit from being placed in a position where they will be protected from the rays of the early morning sun.

WATERING

Rhododendrons and azaleas cannot tolerate lime in the soil, and it quickly turns the leaves a yellow colour.

When grown in containers they must be given soft water with no lime in it. If your tap water is limy, you will need to collect rainwater. Make sure the butt is well sealed to stop leaves getting into the water and souring it.

So long as you have got the drainage right, rhododendrons will enjoy generous watering. If you happen to let your container dry out, give it a good soaking to ensure that the rootball and compost are thoroughly wet.

In times of drought through the summer, you may have to use limy tap water on your rhododendrons, but make sure it is only for as short a period as possible.

GROWING TIPS

127

A Crop of Tomatoes

The humble tomato is one of the most decorative of edible plants and can be grown in any small, sunny corner of the garden – even in hanging baskets or on a windowsill.

sure sign they have been kept too cold – or dead, yellow or broken leaves.

For growing out of doors, do not attempt to plant before the end of spring when there will be risk of frost. Even low temperatures can retard growth and delay the crop, so ideally you should wait until summer which is the best planting time for most areas. If you have bought plants earlier, keep them indoors on a sunny window-sill and water with a weak liquid tomato feed.

Tomatoes from seed

Many people prefer to grow their own tomato plants from seed which takes around nine weeks from sowing to planting out. Seed gives you a bigger choice of varieties, as garden centres stock only the most popular plant varieties. The drawback is that, without the right conditions, you will get poor results. Tomato seedlings need lots of light and constant heat to grow well, so a warm, brightly lit window-sill is essential, as is central heating that does not go off at night.

Sow seed at the beginning of spring. Fill a pot loosely with good seed compost, and flatten it slightly with the base of another pot. Scatter the seeds so they are evenly distributed over the surface. Then sprinkle a little vermiculite over the top, just to cover the seeds. (Vermiculite is a mineral which aids rooting).

Water by standing the pot in a bowl of tepid water till the vermiculite becomes damp. It will darken in colour. Lift the pot to drain out excess water,

A tub full of tomatoes will be a really tasty attraction in your garden. Not only will this 'Totem' bush tomato (left) provide you with plenty of fruit, it will also add a splash of colour to the patio.

Tumbling varieties of tomato are ideal for growing in a hanging basket. The ruby red fruit of this 'Tornado' (below) stand out against the deep green leaves. Keep hanging baskets well watered to ensure a good crop.

Growing your own tomatoes is not only economical and fun – they taste better, too. Fruits that have ripened on the plant have a far better flavour than those picked half ripe to survive the long journey from producer to consumer. By growing your own, you can also cut down – or cut out – chemical fertilizers and pesticides and choose organic alternatives instead.

You can grow yellow tomatoes, striped tomatoes, strings of tiny redcurrant tomatoes as well as the more familiar cherry, beefsteak and common round ones. There are low tumbling varieties that grow happily in hanging baskets, tubs or growing bags on the patio: bush varities, ideal for a sunny corner of the garden surrounded by flowers; and dwarf varieties to grow as pot plants on a windowsill.

Making a start

When you buy tomato plants from a garden centre or nursery, choose healthy looking ones with deep green leaves, and check carefully for signs of greenfly and whitefly. Reject any with blueish leaves – a

Tomatoes make an ideal addition to a container garden. Taller growing tomatoes will require larger tubs; the half-barrel used here (left) is ideal. Simple cane trellis helps to support the dense foliage which blends in beautifully with the lush background. For the best flavour, wait until the fruit ripens to a deep red before picking.

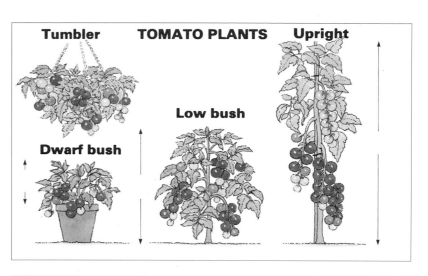

Grown in a container on a balcony, this variety (right) is called 'Pixie'. It is by nature a tumbler but here it has been trained up canes to form a fan shape. Tender varieties like this 'Florida Petit' (below right) are best grown indoors on a window-sill. It tumbles over the side of the pot in a cascade of fruit.

then stand it in a polythene bag with the top loosely tied. Place on a shelf in the airing cupboard for a few days until the first seedlings appear. As soon as they show, take the pot out of the bag and stand it on a warm window-sill in good light but not strong sun.

Pricking out

When the first pair of leaves open fully and the seedlings are just big enough to handle, gently lift them out with the tip of a pencil, loosening the compost to get the whole root without damaging it. Move each seedling to a pot of its own. Use 9cm/3½in plastic pots loosely filled with fresh seed compost. Make a hole with the point of the pencil, and place the seedling in so its lower leaves rest just above the level of the compost. Firm the compost gently, and water by standing the pots in shallow tepid water until the surface of the compost feels moist. Repeat whenever it starts to dry out (check daily by touching the compost with a finger).

Lots of sunshine

As the seedlings develop, they need more light so gradually increase the amount of sun they get. They should not, though, be exposed to sun during the hottest part of the day.

After they have been in pots for four weeks, start feeding them with liquid tomato feed, following the manufacturer's

RECOMMENDED VARIETIES

- 'Gardener's Delight' is tall and upright, producing red cherry-like fruit with a superb sharp flavour.
- 'Sweet 100' is tall and upright, producing fruit, cherry red in colour with a sweet taste.
- 'Mirabelle', also tall and upright, produces cherry yellow fruit with a superb sweet flavour.
- 'Tigerella', a tall, upright plant, produces medium striped fruit with a very good sharp flavour.
- 'Super Marmande', a tall, upright plant, produces red beefsteak tomatoes.
- 'Golden Sunrise' produces medium yellow fruit on a tall upright plant.
- 'Tornado' is a tumbler with small red fruit.
- 'Pixie' is another tumbler that produces small red tomatoes.
- 'Tumbler', as its name suggests, has a tumbling habit and produces very good red cherry tomatoes.
- 'Alicante', a tall upright plant, has medium red fruit.
- 'Ailsa Craig' is also a tall upright plant with medium red fruit.
- 'Harbinger' is yet another tall upright plant with very good medium red fruit.
- 'Totem' is a low bush with small red fruit.
- 'Outdoor Girl' is a bushy plant with small red tomatoes.
- 'Minibel' is a dwarf bush that produces tiny red fruit.
- 'Mixed ornamental' is a mixture of red and yellow, pear, plum and redcurrant shaped tomatoes that are particularly ornamental as well as being edible.

Beefsteak tomatoes (left) are large, firm and bursting with flavour. This variety, 'Marmande', produces rich red fruits on a tall, upright plant which will need the support of canes. Plant in a sheltered sunny spot for the best crop. When harvesting make sure the leafy green calyx is still attached to the fruit as this ensures the tomatoes remain fresh for a longer period.

Produced on a tall, upright plant this unusual yet delicious variety, 'Golden Sunrise' (left), has a profusion of bright yellow fruit.

The tiny redcurrant tomatoes (below) are particularly ornamental as well as being full of flavour. This variety, 'Yellow Currant', has a translucent quality and the fruits look wonderful in a mixed summer salad.

WELL WATERED

- Tomatoes in growing bags and containers require frequent watering. In hot weather you may need to water them twice a day.
- Never water or feed your plants during the hottest part of the day as the leaves may be singed.
- The roots of tomatoes planted in the soil will spread up to 1m/3ft so water the surrounding soil some distance from the plants' stems.

instructions. When the first bunch of flowers appears and the pot is filled with roots (which you will see though the holes in the bottom), they are ready for planting, providing there is no risk of frost.

Planting out

Whether you buy plants or raise your own from seed, it is important to introduce tomato plants to outdoor temperatures gradually. For two weeks before planting out, stand them outside in a sheltered, sunny spot during the day and bring them in at

Tall upright varieties need support. Tie the stems to canes as they grow, and nip out any sideshoots (shoots growing where a leaf joins the main stem of the plant) between thumb and forefinger while they are small. Cut off the growing tip of the stem after four bunches of tomatoes have formed on upright varieties. This encourages fast development. Bush tomatoes and tumblers should not have their sideshoots or tips removed, but use a few short sticks to hold the plants up and stop the fruit touching the ground.

Holiday plans

The safest method is to ask a neighbour to pop in daily to feed and water your plants, in return for ripe pickings. For short breaks away, you could buy one of the semi-automatic watering devices now available. These have a reservoir of water from which tubes slowly drip water to each plant. You can improvize this by using an old plastic lemonade bottle with pin holes in the bottom, pushed in next to a plant and filled with water which seeps out very slowly. Both systems need refilling every few days.

Sink pots and hanging baskets into the soil in a sunny part of the garden, and thoroughly soak the surrounding soil with a hosepipe before you go. This should keep plants going for up to a week.

Picking the crop

Tomatoes can be picked and eaten from the time they turn orange, but the flavour develops more if you leave them to

night. Wait for a spell of mild weather to plant them out.

Tomatoes need lots of sun and warmth, so choose the most sheltered corner you can for them. Patios are perfect, as the reflected heat from the walls and paving helps create their favourite climate. Tomatoes in hanging baskets need a place out of the wind. If you grow dwarf varieties on a windowsill pick the sunniest spot available.

Potted tomatoes

Fill your container with a good quality potting or multipurpose compost. The peatbased kind is perfect for tomatoes – never use garden soil. If using a growing bag, cut the bag open and plant following the maker's instructions.

Water as often as neccesary to keep the compost just moist – not waterlogged, and never bone dry. Water daily in warm weather but in very hot spells, water morning and evening. Feed regularly, too. Use a special liquid tomato feed and follow the manufacturer's directions on the bottle.

PROJECT — BAGS OF TOMATOES

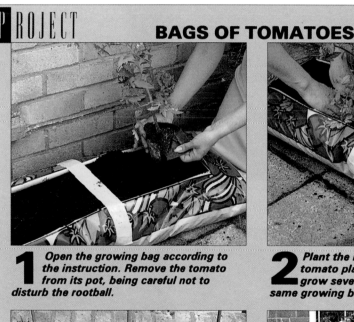

1 *Open the growing bag according to the instruction. Remove the tomato from its pot, being careful not to disturb the rootball.*

2 *Plant the recommended number of tomato plants and water well. You can grow several different varieties in the same growing bag.*

3 *If you plant tall growing varieties you should insert stakes at this stage. Loosely secure the stems of the plants to the stakes.*

4 *Make sure you water the tomatoes once a day, or more in very warm, dry weather. Feed regularly with a special tomato fertilizer.*

SETTING FRUIT

When growing conditions are not ideal, tomato plants may produce plenty of flowers, but not fruit, or only very tiny fruits which never really develop. This is caused by lack of pollination, and can be a problem with plants grown out of doors, especially when the weather is cold (as it can be in early summer). To avoid this, there are several ways you can encourage fruit to 'set' so that the flowers pollinate and develop fruit. Except in a very bad summer, you will normally only need to assist pollination for the first few weeks when the plants start to flower.

- **create high humidity**: spray plants and flowers with a jet of water on sunny days

- **shake flowers**: tap plants lightly every day with a cane to distribute the pollen

- **set spray**: spray flowers with a special spray, available from garden centres. The resulting tomatoes will have no seeds, but this is quite normal

A combination of fruit and flowers can look very pretty especially when the colours complement each other as well as in this border (left). Positioned near a sheltering wall the tomatoes will thrive and produce an abundance of fruit. Surround them with low growing French marigolds in sunny yellow and orange.

are greenfly or whitefly which will suck the sap of plants. Pick them off if you can or, if there are too many, spray them with warm soapy water or with pyrethrum.

Healthy plants resist diseases so ensure you feed them regularly and water daily. If you are vigilant this regime will see off problems like blossom end rot (black spots on fruit), greenback (unripe patches), half ripe fruit, blotchy ripening, wilting and fruit that split on ripening.

ripen fully on the plants. Before picking, wait till they are a good deep red (or deep yellow in the case of yellow-fruited kinds; bright red and orange striped for 'Tigerella').

To pick tomatoes, look for a 'knuckle' – like a bent finger joint – on the stem just above where it joins the tomato. If you put your finger on top of the bend and press it down flat, the fruit will snap cleanly away leaving the green leafy calyx attached to the fruit. Picked this way, tomatoes stay fresh for several days. If you pull them off the plants without the calyx, they wrinkle and go soft very quickly.

Pests and diseases

Look out for tiny green, brown, pink or white insects. These

HARVESTING YOUR CROP

The beauty of growing your own tomatoes is that you can pick them just how you like them. Green tomatoes are excellent for chutney; when ripe but still firm they are delicious in crisp salads; while ripe, soft tomatoes are delicious in soups and sauces.

In a cold summer your crop may not ripen and you will be left with an abundance of green tomatoes. Pick them with the calyx attached and wrap them in tissue paper. Store in a dark place with one or two red tomatoes or an apple. The gas given off by the ripe tomatoes (ethylene) will help the others to ripen more quickly. Check every day and remove the red ones.

Vegetables in Containers

Creating a mini vegetable garden in containers on a patio or another paved area in your garden is fun and full of meal appeal.

Vegetable gardening in containers is a fascinating way to grow fresh vegetables, especially if you do not have space for a vegetable patch. It is fun, eye-catching and provides a centre of interest throughout the summer, but you should not expect to produce enough vegetables to feed your family all year round.

Range of containers

Suitable containers for vegetables include growing bags, tubs, ornamental pots, troughs, window boxes and, for certain tomato varieties, hanging baskets.

Growing bags, which are available from most garden centres, offer an excellent way to grow tomatoes, lettuces, courgettes and beans, indeed, any crop with fibrous, shallow roots. Radishes and short-rooted carrots can also be grown in them.

Old growing bags can be rejuvenated by freshening up and adding to the compost.

Tubs make ideal homes for beetroot and for carrots with deep roots. Ensure that drainage holes have been drilled in the barrel's base. Line it with coarse drainage material, then add clean potting compost. If this is too expensive, use topsoil – but remember that it may be infected with a variety of pests and diseases.

Window boxes are ideal for herbs, as well as lettuces and radishes. If the box is in strong sunlight this will suit most Mediterranean-type herbs, but it will be too hot for vegetables. The limited amount of compost in window boxes and troughs means that they must be regularly watered, or the compost will dry out and may become overheated.

Window boxes near kitchen windows are obvious homes for culinary herbs. (Suitable herbs for them are detailed in Part 24, while Part 21 reveals the techniques of growing herbs in pots.)

Clay pots look good and are suitable for vegetables such as tomatoes, which ultimately have a large amount of leafy growth. The weight of the pot has a stabilizing influence.

Large, plastic pots can also be used, but are not as stable. However, it is possible to grow tall plants in them if supporting canes are attached to

Even exotic vegetables such as aubergines (above) can be cultivated in a container or tub to add variety to family meals. Patio-grown peppers also provide a spicy addition to the cooking pot.

133

GROWING TIPS

KEYS TO SUCCESS

- Only select varieties recommended for growing in containers. And choose varieties that you and your family find most tasty – it is a chance to eat what you like best, not just what the shops offer.
- Choose a bright, sunny or lightly-shaded position, with shelter from cold winds and away from early frosts.
- Plant vegetables with fibrous, shallow roots in containers that are shallow. Use deeper containers for plants that penetrate further into the potting compost.
- Never allow the compost to dry out. Unless regularly watered, the relatively small amount of compost is likely to be either much too dry or too wet.
- Feed your plants, especially if you are using old growing bags. Most plants underachieve because they are not fed or are given insufficient water.
- Look out for attacks by slugs and snails, especially if the container is packed with plants. They love wandering among wet plants.

firmly fixed horizontal wires.

Troughs, either supported on four legs or placed directly on the ground, are good for low-growing vegetables, as well as herbs.

Reconstructed stone containers – either pot-shaped or ornamental – are perfect for attractive herbs.

Vegetables to choose

Salad crops and herbs are ideal for containers, but you can also plant certain vegetables that are grown for their tasty roots or tubers.

Aubergines (eggplants) grow 60-90cm/2-3ft high. Three plants can keep a family of four in aubergines from midsummer to late autumn.

For success, plants need a long, hot summer and a sunny position sheltered from cold winds. Put two or three plants in a growing bag, or one in a large pot.

Either buy plants in early summer or sow seeds 3mm/⅛in deep at 18°C/64°F in mid spring. Reduce the temperature after germination, prick out seedlings when they are large enough to handle, harden them off and plant in containers when the risk of frost has passed.

Support plants in pots with canes, or in growing bags with proprietary supports that do not pierce the bag. Keep the compost moist and nip out growing tips when plants are 25cm/10in high.

Water and feed plants regularly and harvest fruits when 10-20cm/4-8in long. Varieties to choose include 'Black Enorma' (heavy cropping), 'Black Prince' (early and heavy fruiting) and 'Elondo' (very early and dark, shiny purple).

French beans and runner beans are well suited to growing bags, as well as large pots.

The ways to success are plenty of water (but not waterlogging), sun and regular feeding.

In late spring or early summer, sow up to 12 seeds in a growing bag, pushing them 4-5cm/1½-2in into compost. Bush and dwarf runner types do not need support, but when growing climbing forms of runner or French beans, supports are essential.

Varieties to choose include 'Hammond Dwarf Scarlet' (dwarf runner, compact, heavy cropping, non-climbing), 'Gulliver' (dwarf runner, high

Aubergines (above) flourish best when the summer months are hot and dry.

Cos lettuces (right) surrounding colourful red mountain spinach (Atriplex hortensis 'Rubra') prove the point that tub-grown vegetables can be beautiful as well as exotic. French beans (below) also make a charming patio plant.

Cucumbers (below right) are perfect for growing bags although the seeds need initial protection.

yielding, self-stopping, stringless, non-climbing), 'Limelight' (bush, early, sweet) and finally, 'Desiree' (runner, climbing, stringless).

Beetroot is always welcome in a salad. Growing bags are usually too shallow; barrels filled with light soil are best. Use small globe varieties such as 'Monopoly' (does not need thinning; flat, round shape), 'Monogram' (does not need thinning; rich, red roots) and 'Spinel' (round, mini-roots).

Sow seeds *in situ* from early spring to early summer. Space varieties that do not need thinning 7.5-10cm/3-4in apart. Keep the compost moist but not saturated, as too much water can encourage an over abundance of leafy growth.

Carrots are ideal for containers if short-rooted varieties are used, such as 'Suko' (sweet, 6cm/2½in long) and 'Kundulus' (sweet, 4-5cm/1½-2in long). Both are ideal for window boxes, tubs and growing bags. 'Gregory' (crisp, sweet, 7.5-10cm/3-4in long) is best in tubs.

Sow seeds 12mm/½in deep in succession, every two weeks from early spring to the end of summer. Harvest the roots as soon as they are large enough.

Courgettes are small marrows, harvested when 7.5-20cm/3-8in long. Plants become bushy and large, so choose compact varieties and plant two to a growing bag or one in a large tub.

Buy established plants during late spring or early summer. Alternatively, sow seeds at 16-18°C/61-64°F in mid spring, 12mm/½in deep. Put just two seeds in a 7.5cm/3in wide pot.

After germination, reduce the temperature slightly and remove the weakest seedlings. Harden off and plant out after all risk of frost has passed.

Water and feed regularly, especially after the fruits have started to form.

A good variety to choose is 'Gold Rush' (compact, fruits can be harvested when 7.5cm/3in long).

Lettuces are ideal for growing bags. By using several growing bags, and sowing and planting in succession, it is

COMPACT CUCUMBERS

Cucumbers are usually grown in greenhouses, where their stems are trained up and along wires. However, the variety 'Bush Champion' is non-climbing, compact and ideal for growing bags and large pots.

Towards the end of spring, open up a growing bag, water the compost and place a cloche over it so that a couple of weeks later it will be warm.

Sow seeds 12mm/½in deep in groups of three in three different positions in a growing bag. Place three jam jars over the seedlings, removing them after germination. When they have produced their first true leaves, thin each group to the strongest seedling.

Keep the compost moist and feed the plants after about five weeks.

BRIGHT IDEAS

possible to have fresh lettuces to eat from early summer to late autumn.

By growing small varieties, such as 'Tom Thumb' and the cos-type 'Little Gem', it is possible to have twelve lettuces in each growing bag. Restrict larger types to no more than eight plants.

Alternatively, oak-leaf types such as 'Salad Bowl' are an ideal choice if you have little space – individual leaves can be gathered over a long period. For extra colour on a patio, choose a red-leaved lettuce such as 'Red Salad Bowl'.

Tomatoes are always popular. They are ideal for growing bags and large pots, and can also be grown in window boxes and hanging baskets, but make sure you select the right varieties. Growing bags accommodate four plants, whereas pots about 20-25cm/8-10in wide will take one each. When planted in window boxes, set 25cm/10in apart.

Buy established plants or raise plants by sowing seeds eight weeks before planting. Sow them 3mm/⅛in deep at 18°C/64°F. After germination, reduce the temperature, prick out individually into small pots when established, then plant in a container when all risk of frost has passed.

Support plants in growing bags with proprietary frame-works, or in pots with bamboo canes tied to horizontal wires. In window boxes, use small bush types that do not require any support.

Water and feed plants regularly. Remove any sideshoots (growths arising from leaf joints) and pinch out growing tips immediately above the set of leaves above the fourth truss. There is no need to stop bush types.

Varieties to choose include 'Pixie' (fast ripening bush type, ideal for window boxes and troughs), 'Sungold' (sweet and cherry-like, ideal for growing bags and pots), 'Tumbler' (small and cherry-like, bush-type), ideal for most hanging baskets and 'Sub Arctic Plenty' (dwarf and bushy).

CONTAINER SPUDS

Potatoes are a novelty crop in containers. Plant them in growing bags, or in tubs or potato barrels that allow more space for the development of tubers.

Choose an early variety such as 'Dunluce' and plant in early to mid spring. In cold areas, it may be necessary to protect emerging shoots from frost.

Plant eight tubers in a growing bag, setting them several inches deep. In large tubs or potato barrels place four or five tubers on a 10-13cm/4-5in layer of compost, and cover with about the same thickness.

As shoots appear, place more compost in the container, but do not completely cover them. Continue to cover the shoots until compost reaches the container's top, but leave a 2.5-5cm/1-2in gap for the compost to be watered.

BRIGHT IDEAS

Choose early varieties of potatoes such as 'Dunluce' for growing bags (above).

Container-grown courgettes such as 'Gold Rush' (left) are not only edible but also wonderfully ornamental.

Sowing carrots (below left) at two-weekly intervals from early spring to the end of summer will ensure a constant supply.

Ever popular tomatoes (right) are the classic container vegetable and there is a wide range of dwarf or container varieties to choose from.

A Scree Bed

Rock and alpine plants will thrive and your garden will gain interest if you take a tip from nature to create a scree bed.

In nature a scree is a drift of broken rock that has collected over the years at the base of a cliff. Rocks may be in a wide range of sizes from large boulders to small pebbles and even gravel. Scree contains little soil and rain soon drains through it, but nevertheless many plants manage to grow there.

You can copy this idea in your own garden but, of course, on a much smaller scale. Indeed, a scree bed is an ideal feature for the small or medium-sized garden.

A scree bed provides a natural-looking home for rock plants or alpines and is especially suitable for those that like very well-drained soil. You can grow any shape and size of alpine you choose in your scree bed as they are naturally dwarf plants, but it is usual to concentrate on those with a compact hummock- or mound-forming habit. Carpeting or creeping plants are also suitable provided they are not vigorous enough to swamp other plants that are growing nearby.

What is required?

You do not need any special conditions for a scree bed. The soil type or condition does not matter as generally the bed is raised above the level of the surrounding soil.

Choose a very sunny position, however, as most alpines need plenty of sun if they are to grow and flower well. The bed should not be overhung by trees or other plants – site it in a completely open spot.

The style of your house is an indication of whether or not a scree bed is for you. Scree beds look good with modern architecture and indeed are an ideal choice for a contemporary setting. They also look at ease in surburban or town gardens but do not really work well in a cottage or country garden where they tend to look both out of scale and out of character with the rest.

Planting alpines

Make your scree bed more attractive and natural looking by partially sinking a few pieces of rock into the soil. If you can, stick to the same type of rock as you have used for the surrounds. Choose some really well-shaped pieces for a pleasing effect and instal them in groups before you start to

GARDEN NOTES

NEIGHBOURS

Q Can scree beds be placed close to traditional-looking beds?

A Scree beds do not combine well with traditional-looking beds devoted to shrubs, hardy perennials and bedding plants. They are best kept apart from such features and sited in an open part of the garden.
A scree bed will combine superbly with a patio or areas of gravel. Alternatively it can be set in a lawn, as grass makes a natural-looking background. Brush pebbles off the lawn before mowing.

A MOUNTAIN LANDSCAPE

Include small evergreens with interesting foliage.

The smaller scree can be formed with stone chippings, shingle or grit. This helps to ensure good drainage.

Small, creeping varieties look best if planted tight up to a rock, with some growing over it.

An open and sunny spot is ideal for a scree bed. Most commonly raised, it can also be flush with the surroundings.

In their natural habitats alpine plants grow on scree beds. They are remarkably well adapted to free-draining, rocky soil, and can survive in dry positions which few other plants could tolerate. There are many alpines, like this sedum spathufolium 'Cape Blanca' (right), which store moisture in their fleshy leaves. The blue-grey sedum blends so well with the rocky background that it could almost be carved out of the stone but the striking star-shaped yellow flowers bring it dramatically back to the forefront.

138

Mat-forming plants are ideal. Group 3 or 5 of one type together to create a splash of colour.

Rocks form an important part of a natural scree bed. Group some together and position before planting.

Make a hole in a rock. Use it to plant a small alpine, a saxifraga or a sempervivum.

WHAT SHAPE?

You may prefer a geometric shape such as a square or rectangle for a formal part of the garden, perhaps adjacent to a patio.

An informal shape is more natural looking, of course, and is recommended for a position in a lawn or perhaps an area of gravel. An irregular 'flowing' shape with gently curving edges can be very effective.

When creating a scree bed in your garden you should try to simulate the conditions they provide in nature. Whether you are making a raised bed or converting a larger area of the garden (below), ensure it is free-draining and rocky because alpines hate to have their feet wet! If you have the space for a large scree bed disperse the plants evenly. Incorporate a few well-placed rocks and plant the alpines nearby. Include a good mixture of colours, interesting shapes and contrasting textures.

position your plants.

Nestle some of the plants up to the rocks and allow some to grow over them, especially mat-forming kinds like raoulia. As most alpines are small plants, include several of each kind to create a bold effect. Try arranging them in groups of three plants. This may reduce the number of different plants you have room to grow but it will avoid the 'spotty' effect which results when single specimens of a lot of different kinds are planted.

The best planting time for alpines is early to mid-spring. They will establish quickly as the soil will be warming up at this time of year. If you build your scree garden in the autumn or winter and then take the time to plan the range of species you need to achieve the effect you want, you will find that you are ready to start planting in spring.

The best plants

Most of the plants you need will be available from the alpine section of your garden centre. For a wider choice of more unusual plants you can also buy from a mail order alpine-plant specialist.

To ensure your scree bed looks well balanced and has plenty of interesting features choose your plants carefully. Make sure you have a mixture of mat-forming, foliage and feature plants while mound-forming plants and alpines with intricate rosette-shaped foliage can be used to form the focal points of the bed.

When planting, choose the most eye-catching locations for plants you are using as focal

points and plant the others around them. Make sure you do not plant carpeters too near your focal points or your prize specimens may be overwhelmed when these spread.

Stork's bill (*Erodium reichardii*) forms a neat mound of foliage and produces white or pink flowers in summer. Rock jasmine (*Androsace sempervivoides*) is an evergreen with foliage which forms a rosette-like symmetrical pattern. It produces pink flowers in the spring and will only grow in very free-draining soil. *Lewisia cotyledon* has similar fleshy foliage and produces flowers in pink or purple on upright stalks in early summer. It grows specially well in a very free-draining soil.

Choose rosettes

Tuft-like cobweb houseleek *Sempervivum arachnoideum* really looks as if spiders have been spinning their webs between the rosetted, succulent leaves. In winter it is covered with white webbing and red flowers appear in summer. Another rosetted alpine grown for its unusual foliage and pretty yellow flowers is *Sedum spathulifolium* 'Cape Blanco'. It is an evergreen and has fleshy, purple-flushed, silvery-

green leaves all year round.

Edelweiss is a favourite alpine plant and its star-shaped, felted white flowers are so pretty it should be placed in a prominent position. The woolly grey leaves form tufts which spread up to 15cm/6in.

Plants with a mat-forming or spreading habit should be planted near rocks so that they can creep over them adding a splash of colour. The bellflower, *Campanula pulla*, is a mat-forming alpine with tufty foliage which produces dark violet bell-shaped flowers between late spring and early summer. Grow it with the mat-forming alpine pink *Dianthus × arvernensis* which

Narcissus bulbocodium, or the hoop petticoat (above), is an unusual member of the narcissus family which flowers in late winter or very early spring.

This scree bed (right) is in the best position for flowering alpine plants as it enjoys full sun.

Lewisia cotyledon (below) loves a well-drained, sunny spot and so is an ideal plant for a scree bed. Here it is flourishing, growing out of a natural stone wall.

PRACTICAL POINTS

Unless your soil is very well drained, you will need to create a raised bed about 30cm/12in deep. This can be edged with rocks, or mini drystone walls.

Place a 10cm/4in layer of rubble in the bottom. Top with well-drained compost which you can make from 10 parts pea shingle (or stone chippings), 1 part loam, 1 part peat or peat substitute, 1 part sharp horticultural sand (not builders' sand) and a dash of bone meal. Mix the ingredients well.

GROWING TIPS

Sempervivums, or houseleeks, are ideal plants for scree beds, rock gardens and dry walls. Sempervivum arachnoideum (above) is known as the cobweb houseleek as its leaves appear to have a cobweb of fine hairs covering them. It also has attractive flowers.

The alpine primula is another plant which needs a very well-drained soil. Primula allionii (below) is a tiny plant, only 5cm/2in high, which flowers in early spring.

begins to flower in late spring and outlasts the bellflower into late summer. Its pink flowers are delightfully fragrant and it reaches a height and spread of 15cm/6in.

The attractive cup flower *Nierembergia repens* flowers for a long period over the summer. Lovely white bell-shaped flowers face the sun and grow out of a mat of glossy green foliage. Cinquefoil (*Potentilla cuneata*) produces yellow flowers in summer and catchfly (*Silene schafta*) has bright magenta-rose flowers between

With scree beds less is often best. A few well placed boulders and some simple plants create a look which is tranquil and serene, and all the elements of the garden balance beautifully. The bamboo fence adds a hint of the orient and the modern bench complements the artistic sophistication. Hostas, conifers, grasses and some achilleas for colour thrive on the free-draining soil conditions that the scree bed provides.

late spring and late autumn.

St John's wort, *Hypericum olympicum,* is a shrubby plant which makes an interesting change from the more familiar succulent alpines. It produces bright yellow flowers in summer and has a height and spread of 15cm/6in.

For all year round foliage interest plant *Raoulia australis,* an evergreen mat-forming foliage plant with tiny grey-green leaves. It grows to only 1cm/½in high but spreads to 25cm/10in.

Finishing touches

When you have finished planting, the soil surface can be covered with a thin layer – no more than 1cm/½in – of pea shingle. Pea shingle is readily available from builders' merchants and garden centres. Even better would be a layer of stone chippings, which are sometimes available in bags at garden centres and almost certainly at stone merchants. Coarse grit, also available in bags at garden centres, is another attractive alternative.

This layer of shingle, grit or chippings serves a number of

PROJECT
PLANTING IN ROCKS

A novel idea for a scree bed is a rock with little alpines actually growing from within it.

Try to find a rock with plenty of cracks and crevices in which to plant. A popular type of rock for planting is a soft limestone known as tufa. This is so soft that planting holes can be made in it very simply with a hammer and cold chisel but always wear some form of eye protection. The rock should be sunk into the soil by about one third.

Small alpines suitable for such a scheme include saxifraga and sempervivum and also the horned campion, Physoplexis comosa (Phytenma comosum) with its bottle-shaped flowers.

● Make the cracks or holes quite deep and angled towards the centre of the rock. If you want to enlarge them use a cold chisel and club hammer, but be fairly gentle or you could split the rock in two!

● Partially fill the holes or cracks with a gritty potting compost, such as John Innes No. 1 with some extra grit added. Poke it well down with a blunt-ended stick.

● Remove each plant from its pot and gently push rootball into the hole or crack until it touches the compost. Add more compost around it and firm moderately.

● Thoroughly water the planted rock, then water regularly in dry weather as plants must not be allowed to dry out.

A GROUND-LEVEL BED

SHORT CUTS

A raised bed is not necessary if you have extremely well-drained soil, such as one which is naturally gravelly. Simply section off an area which you want to devote to alpines and then plant directly in the soil. Water plants well for the first few days.

PERFECT PLANTS

purposes: most importantly it gives the scree bed a natural-looking appearance. Also, it ensures very good drainage around the plants so that water cannot accumulate and cause them to rot around the necks, prevents the soil from drying out rapidly in hot weather and stops weeds and unwanted seedlings from growing too quickly.

Watch those weeds

Once you have given the plants the conditions they enjoy your scree bed will need very little attention. One exception to this is in very hot weather. Although the plants need very well-drained soil this does not mean they should be allowed to suffer from water shortage. Make sure that during dry periods in the summer you water the scree bed thoroughly, ideally with a garden sprinkler. The occasional weed should be carefully dug out to avoid disturbing the alpines. Be especially vigilant about removing perennial weeds while they are still small. If any do become established in with your plants, paint them with a spot weed-killer, being careful to avoid the leaves of the other plants. Alternatively, dig up both the weed and the plant and remove the weed roots before replacing the plant. To keep everything looking neat and tidy trim off dead blooms when flowering is over.

After a number of years the plants may start to become overcrowded. Lift them out carefully in early to mid-spring. Split them into a number of smaller portions, discarding the centre of each, and replant them.

Although scree beds tend to suit modern architecture, with the right choice of plants they can also add a touch of cottage garden charm. Perfectly placed by a patio (below) this scree bed makes an excellent transitional area between the paving slabs and the flower bed at the rear. Digitalis purpurea, the common English foxglove, stands tall, and graces the garden with its delicate pink, purple and cream spotted flowers.

The following are easy and popular plants for a scree bed and should be available from a well-stocked garden centre. Order more unusual plants from a specialist nursery.

- rock pink *(Dianthus × arvernensis) (above)*
- storksbill *(Erodium reichardii)*
- St John's wort *(Hypericum olympicum)*
- saxifrage *(Saxifraga × apiculata)*
- stonecrop *(Sedum spathulifolium* 'Cape Blanco')
- cinquefoil *(Potentilla cuneata)*

Pot-grown Herbs

Herbs do best in sunny, well drained, relatively infertile situations. In pots you can create these conditions and produce attractive displays.

Many favourite kitchen and cosmetic herbs grow well in containers – and there are several practical advantages to growing these popular, useful plants in pots.

You may not have space in your garden for a special herb area: a single container with the herbs you use regularly will solve the problem. Some herbs, such as mint, spread rapidly in the garden; in a pot you can control their growth. And in winter you can move containers nearer the kitchen or even indoors, so you have herbs at your fingertips.

Best conditions

Herbs do best in well-drained, sunny sites. Pots drain well and can be placed in the sun-niest part of the garden or on a window sill.

Most herbs will grow well in containers. Tall-growing plants, such as fennel, will need staking. You will need to renew the compost annually in your herb pots and repot the plants into larger containers, dividing them if necessary. Water your herbs regularly, especially in very dry conditions, or they will wither.

Herb collections

Herbs are not only useful but also ornamental and decorative. You may wish to grow a collection of different types of one herb, such as thyme.

There are several different varieties of thyme, with slightly different growth habits,

Pots of healthy herbs (right) look quite as attractive as any other foliage plants. When left to flower or combined with flowering plants they can be very eye-catching. The mauve flowers of chives are particularly charming. Terracotta pots enhance and set off nicely the many shades of green.

A tall terracotta parsley pot (left) looks elegant wherever it is situated. Here it graces the corner of a raised pond.

A mixed pot (left) of green sweet basil and purple basil (Ocimum basilicum). The two contrast pleasingly. They flower in late summer and if you are growing them for their leaves you should pinch out the flowers as soon as possible. Basils are generally pest- and disease-free but need a sunny site.

A line of pot-grown herbs flanks the steps (below) in a garden richly scattered with potted plants. Left to flower, the chives and several different kinds of mint will add to the colour generated by the pelargoniums, fuchsia and other flowering plants.

GROWING TIPS

IN THE SHADE

Most herbs prefer full sun but some, including chives, parsley, mints, borage, fennel, lemon balm and salad burnet, won't mind a little shade during the day.

different flower colours and leaf variations. Grow such a collection in a uniform row of terracotta pots to make an interesting foliage or flowering feature throughout the year. Most varieties of thyme are hardy evergreen plants.

You can build similar one-herb collections using rosemary or sage. Both will develop into sturdy, shrub-like plants in pots. Harvest them regularly and you will keep them in trim and prevent them growing too woody.

Mints are another good subject for a collection. Apart from their many tangy culinary uses, they offer ornamental interest with varying foliage shapes and textures, as well as a wide range of aromatic fragrances. Mint flowers add to their ornamental value.

Site the collection of mints where it is easily accessible — crushing mint leaves to

release their fragrance is one of the pleasures of gardening.

Scented geraniums can be grown outdoors in potted collections but must be brought indoors in winter, as most are too tender for harsh weather.

Table-top herbs

The low-growing habit of many herbs is suited to a shallow, wide container, such as an old sink or a terracotta bowl. Such displays are most effective when raised above the ground. Place the bowl or sink on a patio wall or on a sturdy patio table.

Creeping thyme *(Thymus pulegioides)* or Corsican mint *(Mentha requienii)* will produce a mat-like 'lawn'. Prostrate rosemary *(Rosmarinus officinalis* 'Prostratus' also known as *R. lavandulaceus)* will also spread and will trail over the container's edge, offering a flush of bright blue flowers in spring. It needs protection in winter.

For a bonsai-like effect, create a Mediterranean landscape in the container with small rocks and gravel. Use a scented and shrubby herb, like lemon-scented geranium *(Pelargonium crispum)*, as a 'tree' in your planting scheme.

Herb baskets

A hanging basket of pretty and useful herbs can give you year-round pleasure. Sage, thyme,

variegated mint, a strawberry plant, chives and trailing nasturtiums are all suitable for inclusion. Keep them in order by snipping them to use through the summer, flowers and all, for delicious salads.

Containers

Terracotta containers are probably the most visually satisfying. They are also very free-draining, providing one of the basic requirements for good herb growth. But you will need to keep your herbs watered regularly, as terracotta dries quite out rapidly.

To prevent compost drying out too quickly, line terracotta pots with black polythene, punctured with drainage holes. Plastic, imitation terracotta looks almost as good, is lighter in weight and is less expensive.

Specially-shaped containers, such as towering terracotta parsley pots or strawberry pots, make useful homes for herbs where space is limited. A wooden half-barrel provides an excellent permanent home

for a herb collection.

Herbs grown in pots can be trained or cut into shapes that make them a focal feature on a patio or verandah.

Fancy shapes

Cuttings of upright rosemary *(Rosmarinus officinalis* 'Miss Jessopp's Upright') can be trained around a wire hoop to make a circular living rosemary wreath. You can also clip them, when established, into a pyramid shape.

Bay trees, suitable for front door decoration, can be clipped into similar conical shapes, or into graceful, ball-shaped trees. Lavender plants can be trimmed over two growing seasons into ball shapes, as can scented geraniums.

Mixed planting

In a large container, such as a half-barrel, you can use herbs as part of a mixed planting. The silvery leaves of artemisia or southernwood make a good contrast to the feathery leaves of both bronze and green fennel in the background. Cotton

A hanging basket (left) bursting with herbs contains an interesting variety of plants. Contributing to the rich foliage are sage, mints, parsley and caraway. Ideal for picking for the kitchen, they are also attractive in their own right.

A contorted standard bay tree (left) is certainly a talking point. It has been trained to grow like this. Such trees can be bought from garden centres but will be expensive. With patience you could train one yourself.

Pretty enamelled pots add to the enchantment of a herb collection, setting off the foliage of caraway, broad-leaved parsley and thyme (above).

POT SIZES

Rosemary, sage and bay are best grown in large containers as they grow into fairly substantial plants. Chives, thyme, chervil, parsley and savory suit smaller containers. Start cuttings of rosemary, sage and bay in small containers, re-potting them when their roots fill the container.

The plastic column (right) is a 'portable garden', available from garden centres. Fast-draining, it is an ideal way of growing herbs for those with limited space.

Common thyme (left) forms a low bush up to 30cm/1ft high. Flowers vary in colour but appear in early to mid-summer.

A wooden half barrel makes a fine permanent container, but bear in mind it will be too heavy to move when filled and planted up. Here (right), chives in flower and the delicate foliage of rue are set off by the leaves of hostas. Rue should be planted with care and is probably best avoided if you have children. It can cause severe dermatitis, especially if you get the sap on your skin and it is then exposed to sunlight.

The bright green leaves of lemon balm (top, far right) smell strongly of lemon. It is a hardy perennial whose roots can be invasive. Planting it in a pot will contain it. It likes a sunny position. Pinch out the flowers for maximum leaf production. The leaves complement stewed fruit, fish and poultry.

PROJECT A MINI KNOT GARDEN

The base of a mature standard bay tree looks bare and there are few things suitable for underplanting. The right herbs, however, can turn it into a mini knot garden, with a formal look reminiscent of a box hedge around a traditional herb garden.

At each corner of a rectangular terracotta planter set a variegated thyme, *Thymus* 'Silver Posie'.

Along the sides and in diagonals from each thyme, plant dwarf lavender or cotton lavender. Clip the thyme plants into little pom-pom shapes and keep the lavender or cotton lavender trimmed into a mini-hedge.

lavender and curry plant offer silvery leaves and a low-growing form for the front of the container.

Mix scented geraniums and summer bedding geraniums with fuchsias for a central floral and foliage effect.

Colour themes

Choose a colour – gold or purple, for example, – and you will find there are herbs to suit. Golden thyme, golden marjoram, golden sage, variegated lemon balm and ginger mint, combined with variegated rue, will produce a splash of warm colour to brighten the view.

For an entirely purple planting choose variegated purple sage, purple-flowered sweet violets, purple-flowered thyme, purple orach, purple basil, eau de cologne mint and violas.

Basil, incidentally, is only half-hardy and should not be

PRESERVING HERBS

AIR-DRYING HERBS

1. Cut herbs to dry in spring and summer. Mint, sage and thyme should be cut before they come into flower, when their stems and leaves are rich in essential oils. Pick herbs early in the day after early morning dews have dried.

2. Spread the herbs in a single layer on a flat tray or tie them together in small, loose bundles. Place the tray on a shelf in a dark airing cupboard or hang the bundles from the slats of the shelf.

3. They need persistent warmth, 90°F/32°C for the first day, and 75°F/24°C subsequently, and no moisture (steamy bathrooms are out). The time depends on the sappy nature of the herb and the amount of heat – up to four days at the above temperatures and up to two weeks at lower temperatures.

4. Herbs are ready to store when the leaves are papery dry and crumble when touched. Keep them whole when you bottle them, crumbling them just before use.

MICROWAVE DRYING

Herb leaves and flowers can be dried in a microwave and will keep their colour and flavour, but may lose some of their medicinal properties.

Strip leaves off the stems and place them in the microwave on a sheet of absorbent kitchen paper. For extra safety place a small bowl of water in the microwave. Cook on high for 1 minute. Turn the leaves over and cook for a further 1-1½ minutes. When dry they will crumble. Store in an airtight jar in the dark.

FREEZING HERBS

Parsley, basil and herbs with delicate leaves, such as fennel, all freeze well. Freeze them on trays or in polythene. Pack them in old margarine tubs for storage in the freezer. When defrosted and used in cooking they will retain plenty of their flavour.

This earthenware chimney-like container (left) blends well with the brick path in which it is set. It has been planted with thyme in the top and around its base.

put outside until all danger of frost is over. It needs a sheltered, sunny position.

Pot aromatics

One of the most delightful herbal features in a garden is an aromatic path made from creeping thyme or chamomile. If you plant up just one terracotta pot of chamomile and one of thyme you can create a simple equivalent. Rub your hands over the pots of herbs and their enticing fragrance will waft towards you, just as if you were walking down a scented country garden path at the height of summer.

Making a Rockery

A rockery provides a point of interest in the garden and gives you the chance to be creative with some appealing alpines and garden flowers.

The first garden rockeries were intended to look just like miniature mountains (and some even had models of tweed-clad climbers, complete with ropes), so that the plants in them were completely out of scale. As the idea caught on, rockeries became less fanciful, but were often unimaginative. But nowadays, gardeners have moved away from these unappealing mounds of soil studded with rocks and aubrieta.

Today's rockeries are much more natural-looking, with rocks carefully set into the soil so as to provide the same sort of conditions that rock plants meet in the wild, with horizontal and vertical crevices creating cool, damp places for the plants' roots to run in. The soil has grit added to it, so that it is very well drained, to create a real mountain habitat.

Imitating nature

Alpines make ideal rock plants, but rockeries do not have to be inspired by the Alps. The mountainous areas of Britain, or indeed any high ground with rocky outcrops, can provide a model, as can screes which have become greened over with plants on the lower slopes.

The secret of success is to imitate nature, so that you create a true home for mountain plants, which will then grow and flower happily for many years. Of course, the plants you choose should be in scale with your rock garden. You should try to avoid rampant plants that will take over in a small area. It is also best

In a well-established rock garden (left), a colourful carpet of spreading flowers all but obscures the rocks. A stone feature, such as a birdbath, in a similar rock is a happy addition.

The low-growing spruce Picea abies 'Pumila' (above) forms rounded evergreen hummocks.

The alpine primula P. auricula (right) is a colourful addition to any rockery, available in shades of blue, red and yellow.

Few natural colours can match the heavenly blue of the gentians. The trumpet gentian (Gentiana acaulis) (below) is easy enough to grow, but can be temperamental, in some years failing to flower at all.

PLANTS FOR ROCK GARDENS

CONIFERS AND SHRUBS

Juniper	*Juniperus communis* 'Compressa'
Silver fir	*Abies balsamea* 'Hudsonia'
Spruce	*Picea abies* 'Pumila'
	P. mariana 'Nana'
Cypress	*Chamaecyparis lawsoniana* 'Minima'
	C. obtusa 'Nana Compacta'
Broom	*Cytisus ardoinii* (alpine broom)
	C. × *beanii*
Daphne	*D. arbuscula*
	D. blagayana
Heather	*Erica carnea* (alpine heather)
	E. mackaiana
Rock rose	*Helianthemum alpestre*
	H. nummularium
Rhododendron	*R. campylogynum*
	R. radicans
	R. 'Curlew'

FLOWERING BULBS AND CORMS

Anemone	*A. blanda*
Allium	*A. moly*
Glory of the snow	*Chiondoxa sardensis*
	C. luciliae
Cyclamen	*C. coum*
	C. europeum
Snowdrop	*Galanthus nivalis*
Iris	*I. danfordiae*
	I. histrioides
Daffodil	*Narcissus cyclamineus*
	N. juncifolius
Scilla	*S. siberica*
Tulip	*Tulipa tarda*

FLOWERING ROCK PLANTS

Thrift	*Armeria maritima*
Aubrieta	*A. deltoides*
Dwarf campanula	*C. arvatica*
	C. carpatica
Gentian	*Gentiana acaulis*
	G. verna
Cranesbill	*Geranium cinereum*
	G. dalmaticum
Phlox	*P. douglasii*
	P. subulata
Auricula	*Primula auricula* (alpine species)
Saxifrages	*Saxifraga* species and varieties
Thyme	*Thymus* species and varieties

GARDEN FLOWERS FOR ROCKERIES
(late spring and summer flowering)

Ageratum	*Ageratum spp.*
Alyssum	*Alyssum spp.*
Californian poppy	*Eschscholzia californica*
Geum	*Geum spp.*
Candytuft	*Iberis umbellata*
Poached egg plant	*Limnanthes douglasii*
Mesembryanthemum	*Mesembryanthemum spp.*
Forget-me-not	*Myosotis spp.*

to choose a variety of mountain plants – it is a waste of a rockery to use it just for heathers.

Rock gardens, despite being mini-mountain habitats, can come in all sorts of styles. There is such a wide variety of plants and shrubs, including evergreens, and flowering plants for all seasons, in all shapes and sizes, that you can make your mini-garden very individual. The style you choose will depend both on the layout of the rest of the garden and on what other features you may want to add.

Special features

You may want the rockery to include a pond, perhaps with a watercourse and even a fountain. Oddly enough, although a fountain is an entirely artificial feature, fountains always seem in keeping with the most naturalistic of rockeries.

One reason for the popularity of the rockery/water feature combination is that you can use the soil dug out for the pond to give the rock garden the height it needs. However, if you do this you should be very careful not to create a dull-looking mound, which can happen all too easily.

If you have a natural bank in your garden you are lucky,

RECOMMENDED ROCKS

Sandstone A sympathetic, soft-edged rock that weathers well and looks attractive. There are many kinds, nearly all of which are good.

Limestone is an ideal rock, and most limestones weather beautifully. If you choose a hard one, you will still be able to grow lime-hating plants. Limestone 'paving' is natural, weathered limestone, formed during the Ice Age, and a vital home for rare wild flowers. It is not environmentally friendly to buy this type of stone for your garden.

Tufa is a very soft limestone into which alpines can be planted directly, and is perhaps the best of all for rock gardens, but is very expensive indeed. To do it credit you need to be an alpine expert.

Local stones such as Yorkshire stone, millstone and gritstone, are attractive, and are often sold in garden centres for crazy paving. Being in such flat pieces they make rockery building easy on the back and produce a fine, natural effect.

Rockeries are usually placed at the side or the back of a garden, against a wall or fence, but this is not a hard and fast rule. A rockery may act as a foreground to the rest of the garden, with a lawn flowing around it (above). Here, a mixed planting of alpines and conifers gives colour and height without having to pile up rocks.

An alternative solution for those who do not want to lift heavy loads is to use hollow artificial rocks (right). Though conveniently and naturalistically shaped, these manufactured rocks do not weather as well as some natural stone.

It makes practical sense to construct a pond and a rockery at the same time, and placing two or three rocks around the edges of the pond helps to draw the two features together into a single harmonious design (left).

Limestone (below) is the best rock for a rock garden; it comes in a variety of colours, from pure white through every imaginable shade of cream, buff and grey, and weathers both along and at right angles to the strata.

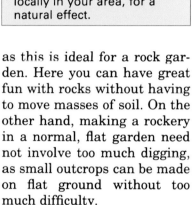

as this is ideal for a rock garden. Here you can have great fun with rocks without having to move masses of soil. On the other hand, making a rockery in a normal, flat garden need not involve too much digging, as small outcrops can be made on flat ground without too much difficulty.

You dig out a wide, shallow depression and pile the soil behind it, moulded so that it is higher in the middle and tapers to the sides. The rise can then become a rock face, perhaps just 60cm/2ft high and, say, 3.5m/12ft wide. This is a very good way of turning a boringly flat lawn into an undulating, interesting one.

Where to put a rockery

Once you have decided on the shape and size of your rock garden, there are some other important decisions to be made. You may have a general idea where you want it, but there are factors that you must take into consideration. Rockeries should, where possible, be in sun. But you could create a rockery as an integral feature of the garden so that where it runs into shade it changes into a mini-woodland garden or even a bog. A rockery does not have to stand on its own as a naked garden feature; indeed the best gardens are those where each element merges with the next.

Although it should be in the sun, a well-built rockery will have its own shady areas, created by the way the rocks are arranged. Some of these will provide quite deep shade, while others will allow plants to have just a little shade in the middle of the day. The flatter, higher areas will, of course, be in full sun.

Good drainage

Drainage is extremely important for rock garden plants and it is no good trying to make a rockery if the ground under it is waterlogged. Even if you build up over it using imported soil, it never seems to work satisfactorily; so it is much better either to have the ground drained properly or to dig out a bed at least 45cm/18in deep and fill it with plenty of good drainage material to provide a base. The soil you use must also have grit added to it to make it drain well.

It is also important not to site your rockery under trees. This stops plants from flourishing, not only because of the shade cast by the trees, but also because it keeps the rain off, with any moisture that does reach the rockery plants falling as heavy drips from the trees.

If you plan to have a pond in your rockery you should decide on the shape of the pond first, and then dig it out. As the soil is thrown up, make sure that

PROJECT   BUILDING A ROCK GARDEN

Some planting can be done as you go along. Put a plant's teased-out root ball on one rock and put another on top, then fill with compost. Otherwise, water the rockery well and allow to settle for a few days before planting. You could put a layer of scree or gravel on the slope to protect the collars of the plants and cut down weeding.

1 Set the first rocks very firmly, ramming an 'alpine' compost – one part sand and gravel to three parts soil – between and behind them.

3 The next layer can curve back into the rockery and out almost to meet the first layer. This creates flat pockets for planting.

2 Curve in the bottom layer so that it creates a natural line rather than a wall. The rocks should slope back so rain runs into, not off, the rockery.

4 Put smaller rocks at the end of each layer. This gives the effect of the rocks disappearing into the soil for a more naturalistic effect.

the subsoil (the compacted soil from below the topsoil) is either discarded or spread out in a layer (never a mound) in the area where the rockery is going to be. This is because plants will not grow in subsoil, and setting rocks in it is not easy. If you do not intend to have a pond, you will either have to sculpt your garden into a hollow and use the hollowed-out earth for your rockery, or buy in topsoil.

The next stage is to use the topsoil to make a shallow mound. When the mound has been completed and shaped to your satisfaction, you can begin to place the rocks in it, starting at the bottom and working up, making sure that each rock is so firmly set that you can stand on it without it rocking. About one-third of each rock should be buried, and the rocks should all tilt slightly backwards.

The brightly coloured, zoned flowers Mesembryanthemum criniflorum (above) are an excellent way of introducing summer colour to the rockery.

Many alpines and other rock plants are spring-flowering. Though you should be sure to include other plants that will give colour and interest through the summer, a rockery can be a stunningly colourful sight in the first flushes of spring (left top).

An alternative to the wild riot of a spring time rockery is to intersperse the flowering alpines with foliage plants (left). The blue-green dwarf cypress Chamaecyparis lawsoniana 'Minima Glauca' *and the mid-green spruce* Picea abies *provide a context for the white flowers of* Iberis sempervirens *and the yellow blooms of the St John's wort,* Hypericum rhodoppeum.

Lay the rocks in layers, or strata, just as you see them in nature. Each rock should bear a good relationship to the next and the strata should meet and break here and there, creating flat pockets of soil and interesting shapes. If you use rocks that are fairly flat, you will be able to make a fascinating garden feature without having to build it very high at all. If you have a pond, you can make a cliff at one side of it, and slope the rockery gently down until it merges with the lawn or a border.

Plants to choose

A rock garden plant is any plant that looks 'right' in a rock garden. The plants to grow will depend to an extent on the size of your rockery and the kind of soil you have (for example, some plants prefer limy, alkaline soil and some hate it). Small alpines offer great variety and you can gradually build up a collection of these fascinating plants. On the other hand, there are plenty of other plants that look in keeping and do not grow too high or spread too far.

For the best effect, choose plants in a variety of shapes and heights. If there is a specialist nursery near you, you

will be able to get useful advice, and the best choice of plants, there. Mound-forming and trailing plants can be mixed with miniature perennials, while dwarf shrubs and conifers add interest in larger rockeries.

Miniature bulbs are at home in rockeries of any size; winter-flowering aconites, scilla and small hyacinths for early spring, followed by miniature daffodils, dwarf tulips and then the smallest irises, and fragile autumn crocuses, will give year-round colour.

One of the most common mistakes people make in selecting plants is to choose only spring-flowering ones. Remember that a rockery which is colourful only in spring is a waste of an opportunity. You can have flowers and interest all year round if you are careful.

A Miniature Water Garden

Still waters need not necessarily run deep. You can create a miniature water garden in a pot or a tub and bring a tranquil beauty to your garden.

A half-barrel pond can stand proud, be sunk in a bed or half-sunk (above). This method gives some protection against cold weather, and stops the water being fouled by earth and gravel washed in by the rain.

A tub or a half barrel can be transformed into a stunning, miniature water garden with remarkable ease, enabling you to enter the exciting and beautiful world of aquatic garden plants.

If your garden is very tiny you may have given up all thoughts of a water feature. A miniature pond in a container will solve this problem, provided you modify your ideas a bit. A wooden half barrel makes an excellent little pond, capable of sustaining a delightful, but ne-cessarily small selection of water-loving plants.

There are lots of reasons for making a miniature water feature besides lack of space.

If you already have a full-sized pond in your garden, you may want to create another,

POSSIBLE PLANTS

Marsh marigold or king cup (*Caltha palustris*) is a marginal plant that has lovely yellow flowers. It comes in single or double forms.

Monkey musk (*Mimulus luteus*) has varieties with yellow, orange or red spotted flowers. It is a marginal that needs to be kept under control.

Scirpus zebrinus is a marginal sedge that will give welcome vertical lines to your design. It is not as vigorous as other sedges, a positive advantage in this case.

Calla palustris is a bog arum with handsome foliage that will bring elegance to your pond. It is a tender marginal, so bring it in for winter or replace plants every year.

BRIGHT IDEAS

Planning a miniature pond is merely a matter of getting things into perspective. A container pond is not going to sustain a lot of plants and shoals of interesting, colourful fish.

Being realistic

A dish in the middle of a table will take just one tiny water lily such as *Nymphaea pyg-*

smaller one to show off more delicate, specimen plants in a formal setting. Or you may use it like a garden nursery bed, to bring on plants eventually destined for the large pond.

Creative containers

Patios and conservatories lend themselves to creative container gardening and a small pond can provide a delightful formal or informal focal point to such a display.

A miniature pond can be incorporated into your beds and borders as an attraction to frogs, toads and other wildlife. It will need to be sunk into the ground so that these delightful creatures can get in and out.

The king cup Caltha palustris *is a member of the buttercup family (top). Fully hardy, it bears bold clusters of golden flowers in the spring.*

An unusual but effective option is to devote an area to several container ponds set at different heights (above). Here, one container grows a tall flowering rush, another a selection of low-growing bog plants, while the third provides a whimsical haven for a decoy duck.

A stone trough (right) also makes a pleasing miniature pond, especially when set in a courtyard garden.

maea 'Alba', for example, and that is all. The simple elegance of such an arrangement will more than compensate for the lack of variety.

It is not a good idea to try to keep fish in a container pond, even one as large as a half barrel. Very tiny fish may cope with a miniature pond but they will soon be lost among the growing plants and you will rarely see them.

Most fish need a large surface area to their living quarters and a fair depth of water so that they do not get frozen solid in winter.

Waterproofing

Wooden half barrels are an excellent choice and so are plastic tubs. Whatever you decide upon, the container must be scrubbed and rinsed thoroughly before you begin planting. If you select a half barrel, waterproofing may also be necessary.

Try filling the barrel with water first to see if the wood swells enough to stop seepage. Leave it for a reasonable length of time and top it up if need be. If the barrel still

leaks after this trial period you will need to waterproof it.

Use a proprietary waterproofing agent bought from a water garden centre or the bitumen paint commonly used for roofing purposes. Use caulking or sealer to fill odd cracks and holes.

Allow the waterproofing coat to dry out completely then fill the pond and leave it for a few days. Drain and refill the barrel several times before you plant to ensure that noxious residues are washed away.

Sinking your pond

Your tub pond can be raised or sunken. If you decide to leave your tub standing on a patio

you will save yourself a lot of hard digging. However, there is more risk of damaging your plants because it may get frozen solid in winter.

If you choose this option, then place your plants in smaller, water-filled containers and bring them indoors at the end of the season.

Water lily and wildlife ponds must be sunken. Water lilies will not tolerate being frozen solid and there is less likelihood of this if you sink your tub in the ground.

Simply dig a hole a bit wider and deeper than your tub. Cover the bottom of your hole with compacted sand and work the base of the tub into

An old sink (above) can provide a home for water plants. Lichens will grown on natural stone containers in shady spots.

A barrel must be planted selectively to avoid over-crowding. A water-lily with three or four foliage plants is the maximum (right).

The sedge Scirpus zebrinus *(below) earns a place in a water garden with its unusual, horizontally-striped variegation.*

MURKY WATERS

Green algae are a problem in small ponds because they thrive on sunlight, warm water and the nutrients found in the pond's compost. Use an algicide bought from the garden centre. If you have no fish, you can afford to treat the water liberally and more frequently.

Remove dead leaves and any other decaying matter regularly. At the end of the pond season, you may have to empty and clean your pond. Fill a container with some of the pond water and place the plants in it. Clean and refill the pond and allow the water to stand for a short while before replacing the plants.

The perfect blooms of Nymphaea pygmaea 'Alba' (right), about 2.5cm/1in across, put it in perfect scale with a miniature water garden.

it. Use a spirit level to ensure that the tub is level. Fill the gaps at the side with compacted sand so that the tub is held firmly in place.

In time, the metal bands of the tub will rot away but the compacted sand will keep the tub securely in place.

Planting

Care must be taken when planting a miniature water garden. You will ruin the look of your pond by stuffing it so full that you are left with a mass of dense vegetation and no clear water. This is not only unattractive to look at, but also bad for your plants.

It is far better to select just a few choice specimens. A water lily and two other suitable plants will look good together. Alternatively, just one water lily in glorious isolation can be

very elegant and all the more eye-catching because it is on its own.

Caution is necessary when choosing varieties as quite a number of water plants are on the vigorous side.

Fairy moss (*Azolla caroliniana*) and duckweed (*Lemna* spp.) are very invasive and will need netting out almost daily in midsummer. Once established, they are very difficult to eradicate.

Irises

Irises, although a possibility, are difficult to integrate into a tub. They, too, can be invasive, but the main problem is that they may grow too tall and upset the balance of your design.

They tend to like very shallow water, which means raising planting baskets on bricks, taking up valuable room. If you feel you really must have an iris, choose very carefully.

As with garden plants, some aquatics are hardy and some will need protection from harsh weather. If you wish to grow a tender specimen in your tub you must overwinter the plant indoors.

Just about any reasonably-sized, waterproof plant container can be pressed into service as a pond (above). Here, a plastic shrub tub is home to a dwarf water lily (Nymphaea pygmaea 'Helvola'), water plantain (Alisma plantago), with its spear-like leaves, an unusual form of water mint, Preslia cervina, and the floating fairy moss (Azolla caroliniana).

One of the most cheerily colourful of all the marginal plants is monkey musk (Mimulus luteus), whose yellow flowers (right) are randomly spotted and blotched with orange and red.

Raised Beds

Extend your gardening possibilities by growing a wider range of plants in self-contained gardens within a garden.

There are many reasons for making raised beds and they are worth all the trouble it may take to construct them. You do not have to be an expert in building techniques. All you need are the materials, some patience and perhaps a helping hand.

Interesting options

Raised beds are not usually very high; generally speaking 60cm/2ft or less is the most convenient height. They can be made of anything that looks pleasant, stands up to harsh weather and will contain soil. This includes stone of varying kinds, reconstituted stone, bricks, logs and even railway sleepers. The bed can be any shape you like and any length, as long as you remember that you will want to be able to reach the middle of it while standing at the edge.

A raised bed is the perfect solution for a gardener who has to contend with the problem of heavy, sticky soils. It means that at least one part of the garden can have a well-drained, friable soil, where plants that cannot tolerate claggy soils feel perfectly at home. They are ideal for growing plants that won't thrive in your garden soil. You can, for instance, make your raised bed lime-free and grow lime-haters such as dwarf rhododendrons.

Make gardening easy

For people with back trouble and other disabilities, raised beds can bring gardening back into the realm of the possible. For those in wheelchairs, rai-

sed beds are the complete answer. The best guide for height for beds for chair-bound gardeners is knee-high to the average person, about 45cm/18in. The ideal width will vary with the individual, but it should be such that the gardener can reach the middle of the bed while parked sideways-on to it. Specially adapted trowels and so on lengthen the reach, but a real gardener likes to be able to

Raised beds are a feature in themselves and also make a striking display of the plants they contain. The material used – brick – harmonizes well with other garden elements.

touch the plants and sometimes needs to tweak an awkward weed from among their roots by hand.

There are many reasons for wanting to bring plants nearer to eye- and nose-level. Some prettily patterned, low-growing flowers, like violas, or others which deserve close study, such as the delicately shaded and feathered varieties of *Crocus chrysanthus*, benefit from being brought up to a level where they can be fully appreciated. It is so much easier to luxuriate in the wonderful fragrance of a pretty dwarf daphne when you do not have to get down on your hands and knees.

Attractive features

Raised beds enhance the garden in many ways. Most importantly they add shape and height to an otherwise flat garden, but they can add interest in other ways too. They can,

for example, be curved so as to enclose bays in which you can put seats or a bench, and a small one can even be made to incorporate its own seat, made of stone, brick or whatever material has been used for the bed itself.

If you widen the end of a raised bed and then build it out in a circle, it can enclose a small pond at just the right level for enjoyment by the chair-bound. For very small children, this will also be safer than conventional, ground-level ponds into which they inevitably tumble at some stage. To make it perfectly safe, fill it with rounded, water-worn beach stones with an average length of 10-15cm/4-6in and then with water. A little bubble fountain will keep it fresh and you can plant it up with water irises, water hawthorn and marsh marigolds, but avoid water lilies as they need an unbroken water surface.

Painted black, the edge of this raised bed (right) provides a neat, almost severe, break between the pale gravel path and a bed of rich evergreens in variegated colours that have been enlivened by a clump of flowering ice-plant. The bed has been constructed of timber and could be made of thick, wide planks or railway sleepers. Wood should be treated with paint, creosote or some other plant-friendly preservative to prevent rot.

On a flagstone patio, a small raised bed (below) has been built to provide a splash of floral colour against a background of foliage. Tubs, pots and troughs alongside it enhance the effect. Stone or reconstituted stone tone in well with paving slabs.

LOOKING AFTER A RAISED BED

The secret of gardening in raised beds is tidiness and preserving the scale. Cut back aubrietas, iberis, alpine phloxes and helianthemums immediately after flowering. Be meticulous about weeding. Plants that wander, like the alpine harebell, *Campanula cochleariifolia,* should be kept neat by lifting sections of them for use elsewhere in the garden. Then fill in with more soil and old potting compost.

Unless you are growing annuals, **don't** be tempted to plant anything for immediate effect. Plants that look great in the first year will take over in the second. Be certain that the only conifers you plant are truly dwarf and not merely slow-growing.

GROWING TIPS

The rough bark of pine logs (right) forms an interesting feature and a contrast to a showy display of pansies. Unless you have the tools, the strength and a talent for carpentry, it is best to get a timber yard to cut the logs to the exact shape and size you want. Take a sketch and careful measurements along with you when you order. Bevelled corners, as here, are more difficult than they may seem.

The circular brick beds (below), built on a paved terrace, are ideal for the disabled. A wheelchair user can work right around them and should always be able to reach the centre. They are not only practical but also attractive. Laying bricks in a perfect circle is, however, quite an art.

One of the things about this system of gardening is that raised beds do not have to be built on good soil. You can site them on concrete or slabs. If you need to keep the roots of the plants away from limy soils underneath, the bed can sit on a sheet of plastic that has been perforated to allow the water to escape.

Near the house

You can also build your raised bed on a patio or terrace near to the house. Then small, scented plants, like night-scented stock, mignonette or even the dwarf strains of nicotiana, will perfume the evening air during a summer barbecue or a quiet moment in a garden chair. Do not, however, build one against the house because you may bridge the damp-proof course.

Why not have a raised bed winding a short course across part of the lawn? With gravel or paved paths along its sides it will make a bright and unusual feature. It is not a good idea, though, if children like to play ball games on the lawn.

A raised bed need not be a slab-sided affair with all the vibrant colour on the top. Planting the sides (unless it it made of railway sleepers) is

DON'T FORGET!

WATERING

Raised beds must be watered regularly. It is much better to give them a good soaking occasionally than frequent light waterings.

part of the fun. If your bed is made of stone, bricks or similar, leave gaps for plants. You can either plant as you build or put the plants in later. Nothing seems to better the really rich purples of aubrieta which looks marvellous in the side of a raised bed. As an alternative, you can achieve a succession of flowering with the shrubby *Aethionema* 'Warley Rose' in late spring and the dwarf penstemons, which are alpine shrubs that flower in

A raised bed can be turned into a small pool or a larger water garden (right). Large ponds can be planted with irises and water lilies and stocked with fish. Add a drainage pipe and tap when building.

The sides of raised beds can be quite as beautiful as the top surface if you grow plants such as Aethionema 'Warley Rose' in the cracks (below).

P ROJECT

MAKING A RAISED BED

The bed is to be built from brick or faced blocks on an existing slabbed patio. The dimensions will depend on what you want and the space available. As a guide, a smallish rectangular bed might be 60cm/2ft high, 75cm/2½ft wide and 1.3m/4½ft long.

Lay the first course of bricks on the slabs. Lay them dry so you can get an idea of what the bed will look like and can move them until it looks just right.

Set the first course in mortar. Make sure you leave gaps for water to escape by omitting mortar from at least some joints at ground level.

For the strongest structure the end walls should tie in with the side walls. You should therefore lay a complete rectangle of bricks as you add each course, rather than building the side walls separately. If this proves too difficult the end walls can, at a pinch, be added at the last.

If you plan to have plants growing from the walls, leave appropriate gaps as you build. Complete the remaining courses and then fill the bed one third deep with rubble.

Fill the bed to the top with soil mixture, making sure you have enough to top up after you have left the bed to settle for a couple of weeks. Add some rocks for interest. Plant up and give the bed a top dressing of pebbles to a depth of 2cm/¾in, or cover the ground with a bark mulch instead.

the summer months.

The bottom third of the bed should consist of rubble to improve the drainage. If you want to grow lime-haters, though, avoid material that contains mortar.

Filling the bed

It is best not to fill up solely with garden soil. You can obtain good topsoil by looking through the small ads in the local paper or ringing round builders, who usually have a stock of it. Make sure it has no perennial weed roots (docks, dandelions, couch grass and so on) and then mix four parts of it to two of moist moss peat and one of sand. For lime-hating plants it is best to use pure moss peat with about a bucketful of coarse sand to the bale. Soak the mixture thoroughly.

The range of plants you can grow is enormous. You can fill your raised bed with petunias and other pretty annuals or grow other small plants such as violets, pansies and primroses – both annual and perennial. Or grow a selection of herbs in your raised bed. You do not have to be an alpine plant specialist to enjoy a raised bed; the idea is to grow

plants that will be in scale with the structure of the bed.

Once you start, you will wonder how you managed without the scent of dwarf dianthus, the delicacy of the smaller primulas, the intricately veined blooms of *Geranium cinereum* 'Ballerina' and the elfin charm of alpine campanulas. You will have created, in effect, a complete garden within a garden.

A bench can be placed by a raised bed or (above) one can be built into a bay during construction. You can then sit back and enjoy the fruits of your labour, surrounded by heady scents.

A curved bed (below), set within a lawn, shows off these alpines to effect. Dry-stone walling is both appropriate and natural.

WINTER PROTECTION

If you want to grow some of the really choice alpines, like the very early flowering saxifrages and crocuses whose flowers can be spoilt by hard weather, make part of your raised bed with one side a little higher than the other. You can then rest a frame lightly over the whole area and take it away when not needed.

You can use a lightweight frame with perspex or clear polythene instead of glass, but make anchorage points on the frame sides or the ground nearby (tent pegs are fine) and fit the frame with simple, short guy ropes from a camping shop.

Roof Gardens

A roof garden can be an enchanting haven in a built-up area. If you have a strong roof and can protect it from winds, almost anything is possible.

Many gardeners gain inspiration for roof gardens from the colourful examples on modern office blocks. These are usually on strong roofs, supported by a steel and concrete framework.

Unfortunately, most flat roofs on houses are not structurally strong enough to support the weight of surfacing materials, containers, plants, compost and people.

Assessing the roof
Flat roofs on houses are usually formed of several layers of bitumen-felt covered with fine shingle with a slight slope for drainage. Repeatedly treading on this surface damages it.

If you want a roof garden get an opinion first from an architect or a structural engineer. They will tell you what is possible, the cost, and how to gain access to the roof from the house – perhaps by converting a window into a door.

Planning the garden
Plan your roof garden in detail and to scale on graph paper. If no view is pleasing, surround the roof with a fence and create your own vista using shrubs and climbers. A bench and cluster of plants in pots, surrounded by a screen forming a flowery arbour drenched in scent, will quickly capture the senses.

All-weather flooring is essential, enabling plants in tubs and troughs to be tended throughout the year.

Bitumen-felted roofs must be overlaid with a framework of 7.5-10cm/3-4in square timbers spaced 75-90cm/2½-3ft

This charming roof garden (above) relies on simplicity for its effect. Wooden boarding, garden furniture and a few well-chosen container plants do the trick.

Foliage plants dominate the scene in this tiled roof garden (left), cleverly giving the illusion of permanent planting.

On an inner-city roof garden, multi-layered planting can create a glorious profusion of colour (above right) and also hide an unsightly view. Stone urns, however, need the support of a very strong roof, although moulded plastic models can make a good substitute.

On roof gardens, trellis (right) is not only attractive but acts as a filter for strong winds and sun. It also serves as a support for hanging baskets of nasturtiums, petunias and lobelias. Foliage plants add interest to the colourful container-grown display.

BUILDING REGULATIONS

Check with your local council to ensure planning and building permission are not required, especially if you want a screen around part or all of the roof.

Some authorities do not allow the construction of any screen that can be seen from the road, or which obstructs the views from other houses. Without a strong surround a roof garden becomes unsafe for children, as well as too exposed to storms.

apart and covered with strong, wooden boarding.

Concrete surfaces, however, can be covered with light-weight and weather-resistant tiles. Avoid slippery surfaces and heavy concrete slabs. Lightness is the key.

Protecting plants

Wind soon decimates plants on roofs – warm summer breezes dry them while winter gales 'wind-burn' tender shrubs, so

make sure that your plants are properly sheltered.

Solid walls and fences do not solve this problem as they produce swirling eddies on the lee side. A lattice-work screen that filters wind is best.

Screens that appear solid, but actually filter the wind, can be created by nailing 15-23cm/6-9in wide boards horizontally to both sides of strongly secured upright posts – but stagger the boards on either side so that they overlap by about 2.5cm/1in.

Most plants on roof gardens are grown in tubs, troughs, window boxes and hanging

baskets, or in half-baskets attached to walls and fences.

One advantage of container plants is that masses of spring and summer colour can be created from a small (light-weight) amount of compost. Use a peat-based compost with moisture-retentive materials such as vermiculite.

Permanent planting positions can be created if the surface is strong enough to take the weight of a bulk of compost at least 50cm/20in deep and 75-90cm/2½-3ft square, and often twice that size.

In permanent planting positions, especially for shrubs and small trees, use loam-based composts.

Container care

All plants in containers need watering at least once a day in summer. Hanging baskets

Make a feature of half-wall baskets by hanging them from a trellis (above). These are brightly planted with, among others, helichrysum, impatiens, tagetes and glechoma.

Be imaginative in your choice of container plants. The unusual Juniper horizontalis (above far right) is an ideal roof-garden plant since it is fully hardy.

Roof-top containers are exposed to the full rigours of winter. Protect their compost with plastic sheeting (above right).

Split-level, lightweight containers planted with petunias and pelargoniums and with the miniature rose 'Little Buckeroo' (right) create a strong splash of colour on this roof-top corner.

suspended high up can be watered by tying the end of a hose pipe to a short cane.

Feed summer flowering plants in troughs, window boxes, hanging baskets and half-baskets every two or three weeks from when flowers appear. Shrubs in tubs also need regular feeding, but not after late summer as this encourages the growth of soft shoots and stems that may be damaged in cold weather.

Winter care

In early autumn, reduce the amount of water given to shrubs and trees in tubs, as well as those in permanent planting positions. It is vital that compost is not saturated in winter, as it may then freeze solid.

Move shrubs and conifers in tubs and pots to a sheltered part of the roof if possible.

Because roof gardens are exposed to the full rigours of winter, selecting the right plants is important.

Selecting plants

There are two ways to ensure success. First, choose permanent plants for their hardiness and diminutive size. Second, grow seasonal plants (temporary plants that are grown for their bright displays in spring or summer) in containers.

There are several ways to create a colourful roof garden. Try planting biennials and spring-flowering bulbs during the late summer and autumn in troughs or window boxes in the garden. Move them to the roof in early spring, just as flowers appear.

Bulbs such as daffodils, hyacinths and compact, short-stemmed tulips (early double types and species like *Tulipa fosteriana*, *T. greigii* and *T. kaufmanniana* hybrids) are suitable, as well as biennials like forget-me-not, double daisies, pansies and dwarf wallflowers.

Some small spring-flowering bulbs, such as crocuses, *Iris danfordiae* and *I. reticulata*, make attractive displays in window boxes and troughs.

For summer colour in containers there is a wealth of half-hardy annuals. Plants to use include ageratum, alyssum, *Begonia semperflorens*, busy Lizzies, lobelia, French and African marigolds, petunias, salvias and verbena.

For plants left permanently on the roof, use shrubs with hardy constitutions. Prostrate or low-growing plants with a domed outline are less likely to be damaged by strong winds than tall ones. Variegated evergreen types include *Aucuba japonica* 'Variegata'.

Conifers and roses

Several conifers with a low or domed growth habit are suitable for tubs. These include *Chamaecyparis lawsoniana* 'Aurea Densa', *Juniperus horizontalis* and *Juniperus squamata* 'Blue Star'.

Miniature roses in window boxes or troughs can be planted and grown at ground-level, then moved to the roof when flower buds open.

PROTECTING TENDER DECIDUOUS SHRUBS

Shrubs in tubs that are left in place during winter may need protection from cold winds. Insert four or five canes into the compost and create a wigwam. Tie their tops together.

Wrap straw around the canes to protect the plant, tying it with string.

This method is better than a complete wrapping in plastic, as it allows air to circulate freely around the stems and leaves.

Specimen Trees

A magnificent, free-standing specimen tree can be an eye-catching feature in both small and large gardens.

A single tree standing on its own can make a magnificent and eye-catching feature in a garden. Plant one to give your garden a focus – perhaps to mark a special event.

Visually a tree can be the most important element in a garden. Imagine a small garden: a rectangle of lawn surrounded by fences; add a patio at one end and flower borders all round, perhaps a garden bench – but somehow there is still something missing. Now imagine the same garden with a tall, elegant tree planted in the lawn, off-centre towards the bottom of the garden where it casts a light, dappled shade across an area of grass.

The tree completes the garden – it gives it a point, a focus to draw the eye at all times of year. You could spend a fortune on a feature to create a focal point – a statue, an arbour, a pergola – when a small specimen tree would do the same job much more cheaply.

Living sculpture

Because they attract so much attention, it is important for free-standing specimen trees to be well-shaped and attractive from every angle and during all seasons. Certain species are ideal for this. Whether or not they also have a particular season of glory, they are very attractive plants at all times of year – with a pleasing arrangement of branches.

In the chart opposite some of the best specimen trees for smaller gardens are listed. Exact sizes are not given, since this depends so much on growing conditions. None of them will grow to be a giant – certainly not within 20 years of their being planted.

The great advantage of growing a tree in a pot is that it can be moved, so that if you change your garden layout or if you move home the tree can easily be re-sited. Any plant can be made to grow in a pot – but some are easier to care for and more able to thrive in pots than others. Check the chart for some of the best choices.

A flowering crab apple tree (Malus species) provides an attractive feature at one corner of a well laid out front garden (above). It is far enough away from the house to be no problem.

POT TREE TIPS

- Never use a pot that has no drainage and make sure water can drain away from the bottom of the pot by standing it on small chocks of wood, tiles or bricks. If you stand your pot in a small container do not let this remain full of water for any length of time.
- Always put plenty of pebbles, crocks (broken pots) and grit in the bottom of your pot before adding the soil at planting time, or the soil will quickly block up the drainage holes.
- Always feed the tree during the growing season – from spring until late summer.
- Water thoroughly, but never overwater. A thorough soaking once a week is usually enough but water at least twice a week in hot weather. Check the soil about an inch or so below the surface – it should be damp, but not wet or dry.

THE BEST SPECIMEN TREES

TREE	SIZE	SEASON OF SPECIAL INTEREST	DESCRIPTION	*GOOD IN A POT
Japanese maple (*Acer palmatum* varieties)	S-M	Autumn	Beautiful slow-growing trees in a choice of leaf colours that mostly turn to yellow, orange or red in autumn.	*
Kilmarnock willow (*Salix caprea* 'Pendula')	S	Early spring	A dome of leafy, weeping branches. White furry catkins in early spring.	*
Young's weeping birch (*Betula pendula* 'Youngii')	M	Spring	Curtains of pretty leaves with a white trunk.	
Golden Indian bean (*Catalpa bignonioides* 'Aurea')	M	Summer	Round-headed tree with large, golden leaves and, eventually, white summer flowers.	
Contorted willow (*Salix matsudana* 'Tortuosa')	M	All year	Elegant tree whose twisted branches look just as attractive with or without leaves.	
Winter cherry (*Prunus subhirtella* 'Autumnalis')	M	Winter	Lovely arching branches spangled with little white flowers from late autumn until spring.	*
Bay (*Laurus nobilis*)	S-M	All year	Evergreen bush or tree that can be clipped into any shape. Leaves used in cooking. (Needs sheltered position.)	*
Camperdown elm (*Ulmus glabra* 'Camperdownii')	S	Summer	A mushroom of large, cascading leaves.	*
Cornus controversa 'Variegata'	M	Summer	A magnificent tree with tiered branches of white-splashed leaves. White summer flowers. (Prefers acid soil.)	
Picea breweriana	L	All year	A very beautiful conifer with weeping branches.	

The golden Indian bean tree (Catalpa bignonioides 'Aurea') bears long, hanging, bean-like pods in autumn. The leaves are particularly lovely in spring (below).

The Japanese maples (right) are ideal for pots. This variety is Acer palmatum dissectum.

Size guide to best specimen trees

S means under 4.5m/15ft high when mature.
M means 4.5m-7.6m/15-25ft high when mature.
L means over 7.6m/25ft high when mature.

Bear in mind that trees in pots will not grow to be as large as those planted in the ground.

Up to you

The most important fact to remember when growing a tree in a container is that it will be reliant on you for its survival. With its roots confined and its soil isolated, the tree cannot draw water and nutrients from the surrounding soil, nor does the soil drain as easily. Rainfall may not effectively water a containerized plant since the upper growth may shelter the soil from rain. Mineral nutrients in the potting compost are finite and

171

RECOMMENDED TREES

Acer japonicum (Japanese maple) (S)*
Acer negundo (box maple) (M)*
Aralia elata (Japanese angelica tree) (S)*
Buddleia alternifolia (weeping buddleia) (S)*
Cotoneaster 'Hybridus Pendulus' (S)*
Davidia involucrata (pocket handkerchief tree) (M)
Fagus sylvatica 'Purpurea Pendula' (weeping purple beech) (S)
Hamamelis mollis (witch hazel) (S)
Ilex aquifolium 'Argentea Pendula' (a weeping holly) (S)*
Parrotia persica (M)
Prunus 'Kanzan' (a Japanese cherry) (S)*
Prunus sargentii (Sargent cherry) (M)
Pyrus salicifolia 'Pendula' (weeping pear) (S)*
Rhus trichocarpa (a type of sumach) (S)
Sorbus × kewensis (a type of rowan) (S)*

will be quickly used up by a growing tree. So success depends on the care you give.

A specimen tree in a pot is a good choice for a paved area or patio and can form the centrepiece in a group of smaller containerized plants. A mixture of herbs makes a pretty and useful feature – golden thymes and oreganos around a potted bay tree for example. A front door is always more welcoming with a pot-grown tree by it.

Winter interest

A shrub with a tree shape, such as a standard rose or fuchsia, is ideal if your front garden gets plenty of sun. When the flowers are over you can swap the 'tree' for an evergreen to give some interest during the winter months – many conifers, especially varieties of juniper and Lawson's cypress, make useful potted trees to fill a space in winter.

Celebrate an important event in your family by planting a specimen tree. You could choose one that looks particu-

larly special at the same time as the anniversary. See the box for trees for each season.

Trees near buildings

Trees are often blamed for cracks in buildings, and while there are plenty of examples of huge trees growing harmlessly only a few feet from buildings, it is best when planting to allow plenty of space for root development in years to come.

The root systems of many trees are as large as the spread of the branches so it is best not to plant closer than the expected ultimate height. There are one or two species that are particularly thirsty, and in some soils this can cause shrinkage and consequent damage to any buildings above. Never plant silver birch or weeping willow within 15.25m/50ft of a building and leave the very large, forest trees, such as chestnut, beech, plane, lime, ash and oak, for the owners of estates.

Planting in the lawn

The perfect setting for a specimen tree is in a beautifully kept lawn; an uncluttered, even expanse of green lawn makes a marvellous, complementary backdrop. When planting in a lawn it is best to remove a 60cm-1m/2-3ft circle of turf around the base of the tree, at least for a year or two, while the roots are establishing themselves, to ensure that the grass does not take water and nutrients needed by the tree and that the mower will not scrape the tree's bark. Later on you may find that grass does not thrive beneath the tree. Remedy this by regular pruning of the lower branches to let in more light. Alternatively, replace the turf with bark mulch, pebbles or paving (but not gravel, which can damage mower blades).

Pruning specimen trees

If your tree is to become a fine specimen you must prune it carefully each year, especially

It is hard to decide whether the mountain ash, also known as the rowan (Sorbus aucuparia), is at its best in late spring, when it is covered with white flowers, or in autumn, when it is a mass of red berries (left). Even in late winter, when the leaves have fallen and the birds have eaten the berries, it is still very pleasing in shape.

Cotoneaster 'Hybridus Pendulus' (right) is another tree renowned for its berries, which look lovely even when frost-laden. At a height of only 2m/6ft, it is usually grown as a weeping standard but can be grown in a pot.

The Kilmarnock willow (Salix caprea 'Pendula') is an eye-catching tree to grow on a lawn (left) because of its weeping branches. Its grey catkins turn yellow in spring. It grows to just 1.5-2m/5-6ft and is fully hardy.

while it is young.

Most trees are best pruned in late winter, when they are dormant. Maples, walnuts and ornamental cherries and plums are better left until summer. Conifers and other evergreens are best pruned in spring or summer.

Use a good pair of sharp secateurs for branches of less than 2cm/¾in. Cut cleanly and squeeze the handles rather than twisting them or you will damage the blades.

A TREE FOR EVERY SEASON

Winter   Holly (*Ilex*) – red, yellow or orange berries; Witch hazel (*Hamamelis*) – yellow, scented flowers; Pussy willow (*Salix caprea*) – furry white catkins

Spring   Birch (*Betula*) – catkins; Flowering cherry (*Prunus* varieties) – pink or white blossom; Pocket handkerchief tree (*Davidia involucrata*) – unusual white flowers

Summer   *Cornus controversa* – white flowers; Weeping buddleia (*B. alternifolia*) – purple flowers; Indian bean tree (*Catalpa bignonioides*) – white flowers

Autumn   Mountain ash (*Sorbus*) – red, orange or white berries; Maple (*Acer*) – red, orange or yellow leaves; Winter cherry (*Prunus subhirtella* 'Autumnalis') – pale white or pink flowers

PROJECT   PLANTING A SPECIMEN TREE

Choose a well-shaped, container-grown tree; then, leaving it in its pot, try it out in various positions in the garden. Check the views of the tree from different places – especially from favourite sitting places.

When you are sure you have chosen the right spot, plant your tree stake before planting your tree. Use a short, strong stake to support the trunk – it should be roughly a third of the trunk's height. Bury the stake at least 30cm/1ft deeper than the tree and no more than 10cm/4in away from it.

Plant the tree in an ample planting hole, adding plenty of organic matter (garden compost, leaf-mould or well-rotted manure) and a handful of bone-meal to the soil under and around the roots when you plant. Plant firmly, pressing down the soil around the rootball with your heels.

Tie the tree stem securely to the stake, using a tree tie. Slacken the tie every year as the tree grows. You can remove the stake after 3-4 years. Water the ground around the tree thoroughly and regularly during its first summer and keep grass and other plants away from the base of the tree.

If your garden is exposed, erect a temporary windbreak around the tree. Use windbreak mesh supported by canes, not a solid structure, which could cause turbulent eddies of air and make conditions even worse. After a few months, once the tree is actively growing and firmly rooted, the unsightly windbreak can be safely removed.

Index

Picture Credits:

Clay pots (far left), painted to match the front door, make ideal containers for the variegated Aucuba japonica 'Maculata'. The effect is stylish yet unimposing and provides the finishing touch to an enclosed porch.

These bay trees (right) have been trained into tall columns and are being used to frame an unusual arched window. The stylish elegance is reflected in the smart white painted wooden 'Versailles' tubs.

For a less constrained, yet still formal approach, this bay tree has been left to grow naturally. The softer outline compliments the country charm of the cottage.

DON'T FORGET!

CONTAINER TIPS

● Check the maximum size of the shrub before planting; you don't want a plant which will block the light from windows or which will look too large for the pot.

● As container plants use up nutrients quickly, nourish them occasionally with a liquid feed during the summer according to the manufacturer's instructions.

● With established plants, remove the top 2.5–5cm/1–2in of soil each spring and replace it with a good loam-based compost.

For quick and dependable results, keep to widely available, reliable plants to achieve the desired effect.

What to grow

Bay (*Laurus nobilis*) responds well to formal clipping, and is ideal to use in pairs by the front or back door. There is also the bonus of bay leaves for the kitchen – but do not raid the plant too often or you will spoil its shape.

There is just one major drawback with bay; it is not reliably hardy. In mild areas, it will survive most winters unharmed, but it is not a good choice in cold districts, especially as container plants are more vulnerable to frosts.

Box (*Buxus sempervirens*) thrives on formal clipping, and is really tough. You can buy ready-clipped pyramids from good nurseries and garden centres, though you will still have to keep it trimmed.

If you want to train your own (which is much cheaper), buy a tall-growing variety. 'Handsworthensis' is a good one, or choose the variegated 'Aureovariegata' for a lighter, more colourful look.

Privet is cheap, tough, and quick-growing – all of which makes it a good one to try if you want to start training your own plants. You will need to clip it frequently as it can become unruly, and it lacks the elegance that some of the more 'classic' plants possess, but a golden privet will bring colour to a dull corner in a way that other traditional green formal shrubs cannot.

Shrubby honeysuckle (*Lonicera nitida*), not to be confused with the climbing group of honeysuckles, is another inexpensive plant that clips well to a formal shape. It is unlikely that these will be available as ready-trained specimens, but they are widely sold as hedging plants, and it is easy to clip them to almost any shape. There is a golden form that is particularly attractive, 'Baggesen's Gold'.

Cutting style

Yew is a favourite topiary plant, but it does not generally do so well as a container plant. You can, however, sometimes buy ready trained container-

It is worth standing a particularly fine specimen of a tender shrub such as this Heptapleureum arboricola 'Variegata' (above) on the patio for the summer. Keep such plants indoors during the winter months or they will be killed by frosts.
A sleek conifer (right) with its tall, narrow shape creates a distinctive focal point near a window or doorway. This easy-to-care-for shrub makes it a practical choice.

grown topiary specimens.

If you want to experiment, and save money at the same time, start with something easy to train like a holly or the winter-flowering bushy evergreen *Viburnum tinus*.

You are unlikely to buy these ready-trained, but if you do not mind waiting a few years, the results will be impressive (hollies in particular can be very slow growing). Both of these plants are widely available in garden centres.

To keep faster growing formal shrubs in shape, clip them with shears as frequently as necessary – this may be as much as several times in one growing season.

Plants with larger leaves

Box (left) is the ideal shrub for clipping and this one has been trimmed into a lovely ball shape. The simplicity of the pot complements the rounded outlines. Similarly, this beautiful bay (right) has been trained into an ellipse and its formal oval outline contrasts well with the easy country charm of a wooden barrel.

Cupressus macrocarpa (below) is an excellent choice as a container shrub. Fast growing and aromatic, it does not require frequent clipping.

The beauty of this euonymus fortunei 'Emerald and Gold' (left) lies in its delicately patterned foliage. Colourful all year round, it is the perfect addition to a patio, path, balcony or any area that needs brightening up. It can be trimmed into shape using shears if a more formal look is desired.

should not be clipped with shears, however.

The least expensive choice for a grow-your-own formal container plant is a conifer. Many grow naturally into an attactive oval or cone, without any trimming. Because many are relatively quick-growing, they are also usually inexpensive. You can buy fairly large container-grown specimens for much less than you would pay for other trained evergreens of similar size. They need not be boring either: try golden forms, or those with unusual blue-grey foliage.

Not all conifers do well in containers, however. Some cannot tolerate dry roots, which is a hazard for container plants if you forget to water regularly in dry spells.

Choosing containers

A generous amount of good compost is essential if your shrub is to thrive in a container. Similarly good drainage is a must. Some plastic shrub tubs come with areas of

SHAPING UP

Pencil column

Pyramid shape

'Lollipop'

Oval outline

Buy plants ready-trained for stunning effects. Use shears for small leaved plants and secateurs for larger leaves.

thin plastic that have to be punched out to create drainage holes. Any container which is less than 30cm/12in in diameter is unlikely to be suitable for a tree or shrub; ideally 45cm/18in is the minimum size unless the plant is still very small.

Plastic tubs are practical and inexpensive but generally do not look very imposing.

Imitation stone (sometimes known as reconstituted stone) is very impressive and an ornamental pot or urn, perhaps with some ornate decoration, or standing on a plinth, is just right for a plant such as a formal clipped bay or a neat specimen conifer.

Frost-proof clay or terracotta pots come in wide variety of shapes and sizes and are ideal for shrubs cut into 'lollipops' or similar shapes as their simplicity will enhance rather than detract from the overall effect.

Wooden 'Versailles' tubs, square in shape, are elegant and look especially good containing bay pyramids. Some plastic versions can look very convincing.

Half barrels make ideal shrub tubs. Before you plant anything in them ensure that they have suitable drainage by

What Went Wrong?

POT TRAINING

Q I have had a clipped bay for several years but some of the leaves look brown at the edges.

A The brown leaves are probably the result of winter cold or wind burn if it stands in a windy or exposed position. Move it to a sheltered spot, especially in winter.

Q I have a conifer in a pot and would like to add some seasonal colour. Can I plant something else in the container?

A Try a few small spring-flowering bulbs such as crocuses or grape hyacinths, and a small trailing variegated ivy. Unless the pot is very large, however, summer bedding plants may be deprived of moisture so water daily. Dead-head flowers for a long summer display.

drilling a few large holes in the bottom. You may like to paint them white, maybe with black hoops. These make attractive containers for most formal shrubs.

PROJECT PLANTING A SHRUB

1. Place a thick layer of crocks or large gravel in the bottom of the container to improve drainage, remembering that it must also have drainage holes.
2. Add a good loam-based compost to a depth that will bring the root-ball to within about 5cm/2in of the rim of the container. Don't depend on the garden soil. Container plants use a lot of nutrients and the soil probably won't have enough to feed the plant.
3. Remove the shrub from its container, tease out a few large roots, and trickle compost around until it is level with the top of the root-ball. Water well.

To prevent weeds, sprinkle a layer of gravel around the top.

Hanging Baskets

Create a lovely visual effect with a beautiful basket that can be hung wherever you need a splash of summer colour. You can buy ready-planted baskets from a garden centre, but it is much more fun to plant your own.

Hanging baskets can be used to brighten up a bare wall, giving a view of flowers and foliage from windows that would otherwise face only bricks. They can make a 'garden' on the side of a house or dreary back yard where there is no room to grow any plants at ground level.

Hanging baskets can be suspended from a pergola to give a floral walkway down a garden path or across a patio. They are especially good in this instance, to add summer colour when the climbers grown on the pergola flower early or late in the season and have little to offer except foliage in high summer.

What sort of basket?

Traditionally, hanging baskets were made from galvanized wire and would be lined with sphagnum moss. Nowadays black polythene is often used instead of, or together with, the moss. The major advantage in using moss is that it is more attractive than black plastic.

A third alternative is to buy ready-made moulded liners of compressed peat and fibre which can be placed straight into your basket.

The basket itself is usually made from plastic or wire and can either be meshed or solid. The main advantage of mesh baskets, is, of course, that plants can be inserted through the gaps, making a spectacular display. Solid baskets,

Basketworks: enliven a wall clad with green leafy climbers (above) by adding a softly coloured basket arrangement; use a riot of red against pale brickwork (above left); a porch is the perfect place to hang a showpiece basket (left).

decorative wall planters and window boxes to your walls. This not only increases the number of plants but it also takes some weight off the floor and creates space.

Even the ceiling of a balcony can be used. Trailers can hang from it and climbers can be trained over it. You can suspend hanging baskets from the ceiling, as long as you can fix them securely enough to withstand winds.

Design ideas

The right design for your balcony garden depends on what kind of balcony you have and what conditions the plants have to deal with.

An ornate, Georgian style balcony, for example, lends itself to a very formal design. This would suggest stately urns and perhaps a statue or a water feature.

Stone urns are out, because the combined weight of containers, soil, plants and water would be too great. Fibreglass urns solve the problem. They are very light and still look good if tastefully planted. Statues are also available in this material, or you could risk a small stone one.

A water feature need not be a weight problem. Self-contained, wall-mounted water features are becoming popular. They are often in the form of a mask or an animal face that trickles water from its mouth into a shallow basin attached to the wall. This brings the soothing sound of running water to your balcony without its weight.

Seaside design

A seaside balcony lends itself to a much lighter design. A bright and breezy look would fit well with the surroundings. Be sure to incorporate seating into your plan.

Brightly coloured, plastic containers are suitably light and cheerful. You could even continue the seaside theme by using children's buckets, but remember to bore drainage holes in the bottom. A concrete balcony will need to have its harsh lines softened; it will always look best when it is full of plants.

Placing containers

If the balcony is a suntrap, masses of climbers, trailers and bright bedding plants will flourish. Gathering your containers into groups produces

Tiles (above) make it easy to keep the balcony floor clean. Here, troughs have been built into the balcony wall.

Tropaeolum tuberosum 'Ken Aslet' (left) is a lovely climber which is particularly suitable for seaside balconies.

Trellises (right) support climbers that will help shelter your balcony.

A wrought-iron balcony (below) is enhanced by a formal display of flowers.

scilla, will readily take to life on an exposed balcony.

Try to make your balcony interesting from all angles – from your window, from the ground and from the balcony itself. Trailing plants can be used as ground cover to make even that level attractive.

Climbing plants help you make the most of the space. They can be grown up trellises and across the ceiling.

Living in the shade

Some balconies can be fairly dark and parts may even be in perpetual shade. This need not be an obstacle if you choose shade-loving plants such as ferns and hostas. These are ideal for a lush balcony.

One of the beauties of a balcony is that you can mix plants that would not normally thrive in the same place. Your shady spot can be home to plants that enjoy dry or damp soil as long as each type has its own container. *Cyclamen libanoticum*, for example, likes dry shade, whereas marsh marigold (*Caltha palustris*) likes some sun and needs wet soil.

variations in height, shape and colour. Such an arrangement is attractive whether you are working with brightly coloured bedding plants or a range of foliage plants.

Containers can be planted with wind-resistant garden favourites such as snapdragons, *Calendula* marigolds, *Clarkia*, busy Lizzies and *Tagetes* marigolds. These will give a colourful display in summer and are easy-going plants.

A whole host of bulbs, including crocuses, freesias, daffodils, tulips, hyacinths and

Sunken Gardens

The ideal way to landscape a natural hollow, a sunken garden can also improve a flat site by adding a change of level, privacy and shelter.

Sunken gardens have a magic of their own. Sitting in one, you can relax in your own private suntrap, sheltered from wind, traffic noise and other people. The best of them are real secret gardens.

Sunken gardens were common features in formal and semi-formal gardens 50 years ago. The traditional sunken garden was a round or square area several feet lower than the surrounding garden. Plants were grown in the stone walls or rockeries shoring up the sides, and there was a lawn, a seat and perhaps a formal pond in the centre.

Informality

Sunken gardens do not have to be formal. The basic idea behind a sunken garden is to plant up a hollow in the

A sunken garden can be a central feature or it can be subtly blended in. If your sunken garden has lots of 'hard landscaping' – walls and beds of brick or stone, floors of paving or concrete – it will stand out more (above), at least until the materials have weathered. The sunken garden (right) blends in, although it has steps and flooring of paving stones, because the beds at the sides are a continuation of the surrounding lawn.